# Cambridge Elements

**Elements in European Politics**
edited by
Catherine De Vries
*Bocconi University*
Gary Marks
*University of North Carolina at Chapel Hill and European University Institute*

# THE EUROPEAN IDEOLOGICAL SPACE IN VOTERS' OWN WORDS

Noam Gidron
*Hebrew University of Jerusalem*

Thomas Tichelbaecker
*Princeton University*

CAMBRIDGE
UNIVERSITY PRESS

Shaftesbury Road, Cambridge CB2 8EA, United Kingdom

One Liberty Plaza, 20th Floor, New York, NY 10006, USA

477 Williamstown Road, Port Melbourne, VIC 3207, Australia

314–321, 3rd Floor, Plot 3, Splendor Forum, Jasola District Centre,
New Delhi – 110025, India

103 Penang Road, #05–06/07, Visioncrest Commercial, Singapore 238467

Cambridge University Press is part of Cambridge University Press & Assessment,
a department of the University of Cambridge.

We share the University's mission to contribute to society through the pursuit of
education, learning and research at the highest international levels of excellence.

www.cambridge.org
Information on this title: www.cambridge.org/9781009565646

DOI: 10.1017/9781009439305

When citing this work, please include a reference to the DOI 10.1017/9781009439305

First published 2025

*A catalogue record for this publication is available from the British Library*

ISBN 978-1-009-56564-6 Hardback
ISBN 978-1-009-43932-9 Paperback
ISSN 2754-5032 (online)
ISSN 2754-5024 (print)

# The European Ideological Space in Voters' Own Words

## Elements in European Politics

DOI: 10.1017/9781009439305
First published online: January 2025

Noam Gidron
*Hebrew University of Jerusalem*
Thomas Tichelbaecker
*Princeton University*

**Author for correspondence:** Noam Gidron, noam.gidron@mail.huji.ac.il

**Abstract:** There is a broad consensus that the ideological space of Western democracies consists of two distinct dimensions: one economic and the other cultural. In this Element, the authors explore how ordinary citizens make sense of these two dimensions. Analyzing novel survey data collected across ten Western democracies, they employ text analysis techniques to investigate responses to open-ended questions. They examine variations in how people interpret these two ideological dimensions along three levels of analysis: across countries, based on demographic features, and along the left–right divide. Their results suggest that there are multiple two-dimensional spaces: that is, different groups ascribe different meanings to what the economic and cultural political divides stand for. They also find that the two dimensions are closely intertwined in people's minds. Their findings make theoretical contributions to the study of electoral politics and political ideology.

**Keywords:** ideology, public opinion, voters, parties, dimensions

ISBNs: 9781009565646 (HB) 9781009439329 (PB) 9781009439305 (OC)
ISSNs: 2754-5032 (online), 2754-5024 (print)

# Contents

# 1 Introduction

What we see in the world depends on the lenses through which we look at it, and perhaps the most common lens through which scholars view Western electoral politics is that of the two-dimensional framework. In this framework, electoral politics takes place in a space consisting of two intersecting dimensions: one economic and the other cultural (Häusermann and Kriesi, 2015; Hooghe and Marks, 2018; Kitschelt, 1994; Kriesi et al., 2008). These two dimensions construct an electoral landscape in which voters and parties can be located, the distance between them can be measured, and the electoral implications of ideological shifts at the mass and elite levels can be theorized and tested (Abou-Chadi and Wagner, 2020; Carmines and D'Amico, 2015; Dassonneville et al., 2023; De Vries et al., 2021; Drutman, 2020; Gidron, 2022; Hall et al., 2023; Hillen and Steiner, 2020; Lefkofridi et al., 2014; Oesch and Rennwald, 2018; Rennwald and Evans, 2014; Van der Brug and Van Spanje, 2009). This two-dimensional framework has become so ubiquitous that it requires little, if any, justification at this point.

Do ordinary citizens perceive electoral politics through the same lens? That is, does the public meaningfully distinguish between the economic and cultural dimensions – and if so, how heterogeneous are citizens' understandings of these dimensions? What policy issues do citizens associate with each of these dimensions, and how does this relate to political outcomes of interest such as left–right self-identification and party support? Despite the ubiquity of the two-dimensional framework among scholars of both European and American politics, little is known about whether and how the public makes sense of it across political contexts.

Our objectives in this Element are to address these questions and, in doing so, to explore cross-national and within-country variations in how people interpret the political space in which electoral politics unfolds. To achieve this, we follow an emerging body of literature that analyzes open-ended survey questions in order to examine how people reason about the political world, the issues they care about, and their political identities (Bochsler et al., 2021; Condon and Wichowsky, 2020; Jankowski et al., 2023; Rothschild et al., 2019; Stantcheva, 2022, 2024; Zollinger, 2024). We analyze novel survey data collected in ten advanced democracies that differ in the structure of their party systems: France, Germany, Greece, Italy, the Netherlands, Poland, Spain, Sweden, the United Kingdom, and the United States.[1]

---

[1]  In terms of scope conditions, our Element is limited to Western polities – although it is important to note that the two-dimensional theoretical framework has been applied also to other countries around the globe. For instance, Malka et al. (2019) examine the relationship between

Our surveys asked respondents about the economic and cultural disputes that shape the electoral arena. We employ several modes of automated and manual text analysis to identify the issues most strongly associated with the economic and cultural dimensions, and then examine variations in the responses to the open-ended questions across countries, demographic features, the left–right divide, and party choice. Focusing on references to inequality in the open-ended responses, we also demonstrate that while the two dimensions are analytically distinct – this distinction is not that clear-cut in people's minds.

## 1.1 Plan of the Element and Key Findings

Our Element begins with a discussion of the theoretical underpinnings behind the two-dimensional framework. We consider how scholars from different subfields define the economic and cultural dimensions and the policies they associate with each of them. We elaborate on the heterogeneous understandings of the second, cultural dimension – as there is less agreement among scholars regarding its content and how its meaning has evolved over the past few decades.

We then turn to explore responses to open-ended survey questions that invited respondents to reflect on the economic and cultural issues that structure electoral politics in their country. Our Element's first set of empirical analyses explores cross-national variation in the meanings of the two dimensions. The two-dimensional framework has been applied to multiple countries, but do the economic and cultural dimensions mean the same across different countries? Should we expect the economic dimension to be interpreted similarly in countries with different economic arrangements such as the United Kingdom and Sweden, or that the cultural dimension would carry similar meanings in countries where religion plays a very different role in politics, such as the Netherlands and Poland?

Our analyses reveal that cross-national variation in the meanings of the economic and cultural dimensions is especially pronounced with regard to the "new right" issue of immigration and "new left" issue of green policies. While about 40% of respondents in Germany and Italy mentioned immigration when asked about the cultural dimension, the number drops to 11% when shifting to Poland. And while close to 30% of German respondents mentioned the environment when asked about the economic dimension, this issue was virtually nonexistent in responses collected in Greece. The application of the

___

the economic and cultural dimensions in mass public opinion not only in Western polities but also in medium- and low-development countries from all continents.

two-dimensional framework for cross-national comparative analyses of electoral politics has proved extremely fruitful, yet our findings suggest that these dimensions can mean different things in different countries.

Perceptions of the two-dimensional ideological space vary not only across but also within countries. To explore this issue, we first examine variations based on individual-level characteristics. Here we find that the age divide strongly conditions respondents' understanding of the two-dimensional framework, more so than most other demographic variables. More specifically, when asked about the cultural dimension, older people are more likely to reference immigration, while younger people raise issues related to LGBT rights, homophobia, and sexism. This finding contributes to recent work on the age-based ideological divide in general, and with regard to cultural preferences in particular (Caughey et al., 2019; Lauterbach and De Vries, 2020; Mitteregger, 2024; Norris and Inglehart, 2019; O'Grady, 2023).

In the next set of empirical analyses, we explore differences in people's understandings of the two dimensions across the right–left divide and party lines. These analyses reveal that thinking about the cultural and economic dimensions in terms of immigration is predictive of support for (some) right-wing parties; on the left, inequality plays a prominent role in defining the economic dimension. While previous work shows that left-wing and right-wing supporters vary in their positions on the economic and cultural dimensions (Dalton, 2010; Gidron and Ziblatt, 2019; Oesch and Rennwald, 2018), our findings reveal that these voters differ also in the policies they associate with these dimensions.

A common theme that comes out of our findings is that the "new politics" issues – that is, immigration and green policies – are interpreted by the public as pertaining to *both* the economic and cultural dimensions. In fact, within our overall sample, issues related to the environment have been more commonly mentioned in the context of the economic rather than the cultural dimension – even though environmentalism is often considered a cornerstone of the cultural dimension.

To further explore such intersections between the two dimensions, we investigate how our respondents reference inequality in the open-ended responses. We focus on inequality following ethnographic work that documented how rural Americans rely on both economic and cultural frameworks as they make sense of various aspects of inequality (Cramer, 2012, 2016). Our analyses suggest that this is a generalizable pattern, mostly on the right. Across different countries in our sample, right-wing respondents mix economic and cultural considerations when referencing inequality. More specifically, they often blame the government for perpetuating inequality by providing preferential economic treatment to culturally defined groups that they perceive as undeserving, such as immigrants and LGBT persons. On the left, references to inequality in some cases relate to environmental concerns in ways that again blur the line between the two dimensions. While the analytic distinction between the two dimensions is useful, it is also important to keep in mind that this distinction can collapse in people's lived experience and how they reason about politics (Bolet, 2021; Gest, 2016; Gidron and Hall, 2017, 2020; Lamont, 2009; Lamont et al., 2017; Rhodes-Purdy et al., 2023; Sides et al., 2019).

Our Element is structured as follows. In the next chapter, we discuss how scholars of European and American politics theorize the two-dimensional space. Then, we present our dataset and empirical toolkit. Since the analysis of multilingual, cross-national responses to open-ended survey questions is still in relatively early stages (Haaland et al., 2024), we elaborate on the multiple decisions and steps made in the process of analyzing the data, in the hope others will follow and improve on our approach. In the empirical section, we analyze ordinary citizens' understanding of the two dimensions along three levels of analysis: country-level variations, demographic characteristics, and electoral leanings (left–right self-identification and partisanship). We then consider references to inequality in the open-ended responses, and how they transcend the economic versus cultural dichotomy. We conclude our findings and discuss their implications, as well as the multiple avenues for future research they open.

## 2 The Two-Dimensional Framework

In the field of electoral politics of advanced democracies, there has been little research as influential as Kitschelt's work on social democracy (1994). In addition to its explication of the strategic dilemmas of center-left parties, this foundational book established and popularized an image of the electoral space as consisting of two intersecting ideological dimensions: one economic, the second cultural.[2]

---

[2] Our focus in this Element is on the dimensions that structure the electoral space – a theoretical construct that is closely related yet also analytically distinct from that of political cleavages. Dimensions are part of the materials of which cleavages are made of, but they in themselves are not enough. As Hooghe and Marks (2018) explain, "cleavage theory claims that the issues that divide voters are connected in durable dimensions, that political parties make programmatic commitments on these issue dimensions, and that as a result of issue coherence and programmatic stickiness, change in party systems is a punctuated process that arises from shocks external to the party system" (p. 10). According to Bartolini (2000), "the concept of cleavage can be seen to incorporate three dimensions: an empirical element, which identifies the empirical referent of the concept and which we can define in socio-structural terms; a normative element, that is, the set of values and beliefs that provides a sense of identity and role to the empirical element and reflects the self-awareness of the social group(s) involved; and an organizational/behavioral element, that is, the set of individual interactions, institutions,

Over the last three decades, this two-dimensional framework has proved highly generative for research on the evolution of electoral politics and the strategies of political parties. Following Kitschelt's work, research on social democracy has relied heavily on this understanding of the electoral space in order to explore the successes and failures of center-left parties (Abou-Chadi and Wagner, 2020; Bremer and Rennwald, 2023; Rennwald and Evans, 2014). Since then, and as further discussed in Section 2.1, this theoretical construct of a two-dimensional space has been extended to the study of virtually all party families and has dominated debates about the evolution of Western electoral politics (Dassonneville et al., 2023; Gethin et al., 2022; Gonthier and Guerra, 2023; Koedam, 2022; Kriesi et al., 2008; Oesch and Rennwald, 2018). Considering how ubiquitous this framework has become, it is worth taking a closer look at its building blocks: that is, how scholars theorize the two dimensions that together construct the electoral space.

The economic dimension, in Kitschelt's terms, ranges from "socialist politics" to "capitalist politics." This dimension pertains to state intervention in the economy, broadly construed: from taxation and redistribution to the regulation of businesses. This is the axis of material contestation over – in Lasswell's memorable phrase – "Who Gets What, When, How." This dimension of politics, which traces its roots to the Industrial Revolution (Lipset and Rokkan, 1990), dominated the electoral arena around the mid-twentieth century. It shaped the politics of welfare state formation, as center-left parties represented workers' demands for a more generous welfare state against center-right parties whose upper middle-class supporters were more cautious about state intervention in the economy (Hall, 2013). Smaller, agrarian parties – which were especially influential in shaping the Nordic welfare regime – also represented economic interests, those of the agrarian sector (Manow, 2009). Influential studies of electoral politics have centered on this economic dimension, assuming that voters' orientations on economic policymaking, derived from their economic position, are the primary driver of voting (Iversen and Soskice, 2006).

The economic dimension captures citizens' orientations toward state intervention in the economy, and the specific policies most relevant to it have adapted over time to changes in the structure of the economy. Scholars distinguish between at least two subcomponents of the economic dimension:

---

and organizations, such as political parties, that develop, as part of the cleavage" (pp. 16–17). The concept of cleavage is thus more expansive and requires a broader perspective than this Element's focus on ideological dimensions.

consumption and investment. Consumption policies refer to traditional welfare transfers, such as pensions, that provide short-term returns, while investment policies incorporate education and childcare spending for the long-term development of human capital – issues that have risen in importance over time, following the transition from the industrial to the knowledge economy (Beramendi et al., 2015; Häusermann et al., 2022). This is to say, there are good reasons to think of the economic dimension as one that contains multitudes and has not remained frozen over the years. Nevertheless, at their core, its various components all relate to struggles over different forms of material resources.

The second, cultural dimension is somewhat harder to define: its content is more contested and potentially also more dynamic over time. As a result, there is also no consensus about how to label this dimension and its opposing poles. In Kitschelt's terms, the cultural dimension ranges from libertarian to authoritarian values. The terminology here could be slightly confusing: libertarianism in this context stands for "individual autonomy in shaping personal and collective identities, the transformation of gender roles, and an ethic of enjoyment rather than of accumulation and order" (Kitschelt, 1994, 22–23); this is very different from the American meaning of the term, which commonly denotes a right-wing pro-market ideology (Kersch, 2011). At the other end of this dimension is the authoritarian pole, whose definition goes back to works on the authoritarian personality and its emphasis on compliance, authority, hierarchy, and order (Adorno et al., 1950; Stenner, 2005).

The specific policies scholars associate with the second, cultural dimension have changed over time. Originally defined in terms of religious orientations versus secularism, the rise of new social movements in the 1960s infused it with post-materialist values such as feminism and environmentalism (Kitschelt and Hellemans, 1990). This shift was a result of a "silent revolution" in Western politics, which has taken place as citizens born into a prosperous environment came to adopt post-material values (Inglehart and Flanagan, 1987).

Then, following the rise of globalization in general and European integration in particular during the 1990s, the second dimension was again redefined. Hooghe et al. (2002) argue that around this time, the second dimension came to be associated not only with contrasting ethical judgments of different lifestyles but also specifically with views on immigration and national identity. Thus, they define this dimension as "ranging from Green-alternative-libertarian (GAL) to traditional-authoritarian-nationalist (TAN)." The GAL pole of this dimension, where green parties are located, is defined by commitment to environmentalism and cross-national integration – while the TAN pole, where radical right parties are located, is defined by opposition to immigration and rejection of cosmopolitanism.

Closely related, Kriesi et al. (2006, 2008) argue that the rise of globalization has redefined the second dimension so that it now ranges between demarcation and integration, that is from a conservative emphasis on the protection of national cultures to progressive universalism. In this formulation, the second dimension captures different conceptions of the community (Bornschier, 2010b): on one side of the cultural dimension, we find globalization losers, whose life prospects have diminished and thus hold to the demarcation of national boundaries, while the other side is occupied by globalization winners, who are well equipped to deal with a globalized world and express cosmopolitan values. With their emphasis on the cultural dimension as capturing disagreements over national boundaries, these interpretations of the second dimension (GAL-TAN, demarcation-integration) have been useful specifically, though not exclusively, in the study of anti-immigration radical right parties (Abou-Chadi et al., 2022; Bornschier, 2010a; Lefkofridi et al., 2014; Norris and Inglehart, 2019; Spies and Franzmann, 2011).

Commenting on the fluidity of the content attached to this second dimension, as well as how it is differently labeled by different scholars, Hooghe and Marks (2018, 123) summarize this body of literature as follows:

> In much of Europe the crises have reinforced a new transnational cleavage that has at its core a cultural conflict pitting libertarian, universalistic values against the defense of nationalism and particularism (Bornschier and Kriesi 2012; Golder 2016: 488; Höglinger 2016). Recent literature has spawned a variety of concepts to describe this: demarcation vs integration (Kriesi et al. 2006, 2012); libertarian-universalistic vs traditionalist-communitarian (Bornschier 2010); universalism vs particularism (Beramendi et al. 2015; Häusermann and Kriesi 2015); cosmopolitan vs communitarian (Teney et al. 2014); and GAL vs TAN (Hooghe et al. 2002).

While Kitschelt's work, as well as most of the other research already mentioned, centered on European politics with its multiparty systems,[3] scholars of American politics have also defined the ideological space as two-dimensional (Jost et al., 2009). In their review of research on American ideology, Carmines and D'Amico (2015, 212) refer to a distinction between the economic dimension and a "social dimension" that relates to "issues like abortion, same-sex marriage, and the role of religion in public affairs." Closely

---

[3] For a closely related discussion of different conceptualizations of the second dimension, see Ford and Jennings (2020). These authors also consider the role of geography and place-based identity in shaping the content of the second dimension, following Rodden (2019).

related, in his discussion of party competition in the United States, Drutman (2020) follows this path and considers political battles over who gets what (the economic dimension) and who we are (the cultural dimension). Table 1 summarizes these key conceptualizations of the two-dimensional framework across the European and American contexts, at varying levels of abstraction.[4]

## 2.1  Identifying the Two Dimensions at the Mass Level

In their efforts to identify and measure the two dimensions in the electorate, scholars commonly analyze survey data using dimension reduction methods.[5] In these analyses, scholars identify a set of relevant survey questions and demonstrate that tools such as factor analysis can detect two dimensions that correspond to the broad categories of economic and cultural issues (Gidron, 2022; Hall et al., 2023; Häusermann and Kriesi, 2015; Hillen and Steiner, 2020). Alternatively, another approach to locate voters within the ideological space is for scholars to decide a priori which survey question relates to which of the two dimensions (Lefkofridi et al., 2014). This body of research has provided important insights into the landscape of mass preferences on which parties compete; yet it is not without limitations.

First, these analyses often require scholars to set in advance whether the dimensions are orthogonal and whether a certain policy issue can be associated with only one of the dimensions or with both of them (Hall et al., 2023, 9). However, this issue should supposedly be determined inductively and may vary cross-nationally (Dolezal et al., 2013).

Second, the boundaries between the economic and cultural dimensions may be more porous than the discussion (see Table 1) suggests (Cramer, 2016; Gidron and Hall, 2017; Sides et al., 2019). That is, certain policy issues may lie at the intersection of economic and cultural concerns. As Häusermann and Kriesi (2015) observe, "issues such as welfare chauvinism

---

[4]  We note that there are also conceptualizations of the ideological space as consisting of three, rather than just two, dimensions. Kitschelt and Rehm (2014), for instance, distinguish between the three following dimensions: greed (the economic dimension), grid (libertarianism versus authoritarianism), and group (immigration). Focusing on the American context, Baldassarri and Goldberg (2014) identify four dimensions: economics, civil rights, morality, and foreign policy. In this Element, we focus exclusively on the two-dimensional understanding of the ideological space both since we perceive it as much more common in the field of European electoral politics, and because our data-collection efforts focused on these two dimensions.

[5]  Scholars have also developed tools to locate parties within the two-dimensional space, based on data sources such as expert surveys (Van der Brug and Van Spanje, 2009) or content analyses of daily newspapers (Kriesi et al., 2006). We pay less attention to the measurement of parties' positions on these dimensions as we are theoretically interested in how these dimensions are understood at the mass level.

**Table 1** Conceptualizations of the two-dimensional space

| | Economic dimension | Cultural dimension |
|---|---|---|
| Kitschelt (1994) | From "Planned allocation of resources" to "markets and free exchange, capitalism" | From "self-organized community" to "paternalism and corporatism" |
| Hooghe et al. (2002) | "greater versus lesser government regulation of market outcomes" | "Green/alternative/libertarian to traditional/ authoritarian/nationalist" |
| Kriesi et al. (2008) | "A neoliberal free trade position is opposed to a position in favour of protecting the national markets" | "A universalist, multiculturalist or cosmopolitan position is opposing a position in favour of protecting the national culture and citizenship in its civic, political and social sense" |
| Carmines and D'Amico (2015) | "What is the appropriate degree of government intervention in the economy?" | "To what extent do current hierarchical structures need to be preserved or altered?" |
| Drutman (2020) | Who gets what: "economics and the distribution of material resources" | Who we are: "national identity, culture, and social group hierarchy" |
| Gethin et al. (2022) | "divides over economic policy and inequality" | "issues such as law and order, the environment, multiculturalism, or immigration" |

or the unequal effects of welfare states on men and women have a strong cultural connotation and are related to issues such as immigration or universalism/particularism" (p. 202). Closely related, immigration may be shaped by economic considerations (Dancygier and Donnelly, 2013; Malhotra et al., 2013) as well as cultural concerns (Hainmueller and Hopkins, 2014). Evidence suggests that mainstream parties have responded to the growing salience of immigration in electoral politics by "increasingly addressing the issue through *cultural* frames without neglecting its *economic* aspects" (Dancygier and Margalit, 2020, 737, emphasis added). Environmental policies are another example of issues that may not be easily classified as either economic or cultural, as they carry distributive implications but also reflect cultural values (Diamond, 2023). There is tension between studies that categorize environmental concerns as a component of the cultural dimension (Hall et al., 2023, 64) and those that emphasize the pocketbook implications of green policies (Colantone et al., 2024).

Third, this empirical approach overlooks potential within-dimension heterogeneity: It is insensitive to the possibility that the economic and cultural dimensions may mean different things to different people in different countries. That is, out of the long list of policies already mentioned, some may prove consequential in shaping the ideological space in some countries but not in others. To explore this set of issues, we analyze how people make sense of the economic and cultural dimensions in their own words. But before that, we present the novel dataset we are analyzing and discuss our automated text-based empirical approach.

## 3 Data and Methods

In this section, we present the dataset we will be analyzing for the remainder of this Element and elaborate on our empirical strategy. Since research that relies on automated textual analyses of open-ended questions in large-scale multicountry surveys is in relatively early stages, we elaborate on our methodological choices in some detail. Readers who are less interested in the methodological aspects of our work are invited to skip this section and proceed directly to the results.

### 3.1 Data

We follow an emerging body of literature that uses open-ended survey questions to understand how people make sense of politics. For instance, in their study of status comparisons, Condon and Wichowsky (2020) use open-ended questions to investigate how Americans compare themselves to other social groups when thinking about economic inequality. Analyzing partisan identities in Switzerland, Zollinger (2024) takes advantage of open-ended questions to inquire identity-based cleavages separating far-right and new-left voters. Others have used open-ended questions to examine partisan stereotypes in contexts as diverse as the United States (Rothschild et al., 2019) and Israel (Gidron et al., 2022). Open-ended questions have also proved useful in better understanding how people reason about economic issues such as taxation (Ferrario and Stantcheva, 2022), trade (Stantcheva, 2022), and perceptions of good jobs (Rodrik and Stantcheva, 2021). Turning to elites, Jankowski et al. (2023) examine how German parliamentary candidates interpret the left–right ideological dimension. While these are all single country studies, we expand this approach to analyze open-ended survey responses collected across countries.

Compared to standard survey questions that ask respondents to select a response from a predefined list of options, open-ended questions provide respondents with greater flexibility to express their worldviews, identities, and preferences in their own words (Haaland et al., 2024). Thus, the analysis of open-ended questions borrows from ethnography the aspiration "to glean the meaning that the people under study attribute to their social and political reality" (Schatz, 2009, 5). Yet while ethnographic research is limited in generalizability, advances in multilingual automated text analysis make it possible to analyze responses to open-ended survey questions collected in multicountry representative samples (Lucas et al., 2015).

In the analyses in Section 4, we make use of novel survey data collected online through the survey firm Latana (formerly called Delia Research). The surveys were fielded online in the following ten countries: the United States, Sweden, Poland, the Netherlands, Italy, Greece, the United Kingdom, France, Spain, and Germany. These countries vary significantly in their electoral institutions and range from the majoritarian two-party American context to the highly proportional and fragmented Dutch electoral arena (Bormann and Golder, 2013). The two-dimensional framework has been applied to all of these cases, making them theoretically relevant to the empirical analyses we present in Section 4.

Fieldwork took place during June–July 2021, with around 1,000 respondents in each country. In each country, our sample of respondents is balanced on current population distributions with weights on key demographics (age, gender, and rural–urban environment).[6] We randomly assigned one-third of the

---

[6] For additional information on this dataset, see Tichelbaecker et al. (2023). As explained, "rather than drawing from a preexisting panel, Latana recruits respondents through partner websites. Once a respondent opts in, they complete a pre-screening survey based on the survey's targeting criteria to allow for the application of survey quotas … To incentivize participation, respondents receive small non-monetary incentives specific to the partner websites (for example, in-app currencies)."

**Table 2** Descriptive summary of respondents' characteristics

|  | Cultural dimension | | | Economic dimension | |
|---|---|---|---|---|---|
|  | N | Mean | SD | Mean | SD |
| Age | 7,065 | 40.3 | 12.8 | 40.5 | 13 |
| Female (in %) | 7,065 | 50.7 | 50 | 48.6 | 50 |
| High education (in %) | 7,065 | 41.3 | 49.2 | 42.1 | 49.4 |
| Medium education (in %) | 7,065 | 40.4 | 49.1 | 40.3 | 49.1 |
| Low education (in %) | 7,065 | 14.7 | 35.4 | 14.4 | 35.1 |
| High income (in %) | 7,065 | 14.8 | 35.5 | 14.9 | 35.7 |
| Medium income (in %) | 7,065 | 20.3 | 40.2 | 21.8 | 41.3 |
| Low income (in %) | 7,065 | 55.4 | 49.7 | 53.5 | 49.9 |
| Rural (in %) | 7,065 | 28 | 44.9 | 26.6 | 44.2 |
| Left–right scale | 7,065 | 5.2 | 2.6 | 5.2 | 2.6 |

**Note:** This table provides descriptive summaries of respondents' socio-demographic characteristics separately for those asked about the economic and cultural dimensions.

respondents in each country to an open-ended question on the economic dimension and another third to an open-ended question on the cultural dimension; the last third was asked a question unrelated to the research discussed in this manuscript. Table 2 presents descriptive statistics of respondents' characteristics in the cultural and economic dimension conditions, demonstrating that samples were balanced across the two groups. Note that for household income we include 681 respondents who preferred not to report their household income.

We used the following open-ended questions to capture respondents' understanding of the two ideological dimensions. With regard to the economic dimension, respondents were asked: "The last few years have witnessed dramatic political developments. Specifically, parties have clashed over economic issues such as taxes, economic inequality and the welfare state. Different parties hold very different views on these important issues. Can you describe to us what you think are the key economic issues on which different parties disagree?" Then, respondents were asked a similar question pertaining to the cultural dimension: "The last few years have witnessed dramatic political developments. Specifically, parties have clashed over cultural issues such multiculturalism, immigration and national identity. Different parties hold very different views on these important issues. Can you describe to us what you think are the key cultural issues on which different parties disagree?" People were invited to share with us their thoughts in their own words.

As we further discuss next, clearly the wording of these questions primed people to mention some policy issues but not others. While this complicates an interpretation of these aggregate descriptive statistics, we take advantage of the fact that all participants read the *same* prompts. This allows us to unpack substantive variations across and within countries in people's interpretations of the economic and cultural dimensions and the specific policies they associate with each of them.

## 3.2 Methods

We pursue a theoretically driven descriptive research path (Gerring, 2012), in which we identify respondents' understanding of the economic and cultural dimensions, and then examine how these vary across countries, socio-demographic features, the left–right divide, and partisan identities. We begin with translating each response into English via the translation service DeepL. We manually verified the accuracy of DeepL translations for a subset of open-ended responses. While the translations were overall accurate, a few responses could not be translated due to spelling errors. We removed stop words and used the remaining words in the subsequent analyses.

Once we have our dataset ready, we proceed with the following steps. First, we use keyness statistics to explore terms that are distinct for the economic and cultural dimension respectively. This allows us to make sure respondents raise different issues in responses to the different questions, providing face validity to our survey instrument. Second, we separately run topic models on responses to the two open-ended survey questions using bidirectional encoder representations from transformers [BERT]. Bidirectional encoder representations from transformers is a method for analyzing large-scale corpora that is sensitive to word order (Devlin et al., 2018) and semantic relationships between words (Grootendorst, 2022), unlike other common approaches in political science to text analysis, such as Structural Topic Models (Roberts et al., 2014). This feature makes BERT especially appealing to social scientists interested in nuanced textual expressions (Bonikowski et al. 2022; Vicinanza et al. 2023).

While BERT is commonly applied to classification tasks, we take advantage of BERTopic (Grootendorst, 2022), which utilizes BERT for topic modeling. This is especially useful for our study given that open-ended responses tend to be short, which poses challenges for topic modeling algorithms like LDA. Using BERTopic and without setting a predetermined number of topics, we identify ninety-six topics in responses to the questions about the economic dimension and ninety-two topics in responses to the question about the cultural dimension (see Figures B.1 and B.2 in the appendix).

Third, in order to develop a more manageable coding scheme, we aggregate these topics into broad categories. For the cultural dimension, we identify five categories: immigration, integration, traditional morality, environment, and welfare services. The immigration category includes words that deal with the movement of individuals across borders, and cover nexts to immigration-related words also words such as "refugees" and "fugitive." The category of integration deals with notions of diversity, national identity, and inclusion versus exclusion of social groups. While integration is substantively related to that of immigration, it is analytically distinct (Givens and Luedtke, 2005) and pertains also to debates regarding local minorities. The category of traditional morality covers issues related to traditional versus more libertarian values and specifically sexual identities, which could be broadly understood as post-materialist values. It may be surprising that the category of welfare services appears in our analyses of the cultural dimension, yet we do find in respondents' description of the cultural dimension references to healthcare, education systems, and pensions. Lastly, the environment category is defined by words such as "green" and "energy." Table 3 provides examples for each category of the cultural dimension.

For the economic dimension, we identify the following five categories: inequality, welfare services, labor market, immigration, and environmental policies. The category of inequality applies not only to direct reference to economic inequities but also to taxing the wealthy and corporations. Next, the category of welfare services covers issues such as healthcare, pensions, and education. The category of labor market covers the relationship between employers and employees, salaries and union membership. The immigration category pertains, as with the cultural dimension, to foreigners broadly construed and includes references to refugees and borders more generally. Lastly, the environment category relates to issues such as sustainable green energy sources. Table 4 provides examples of each category.

Table 5 presents key descriptive statistics of replies to these two questions. Open-ended replies in the two conditions were similar in length: the average number of words in the cultural and economic dimensions was 4.61 and 4.54, respectively.

Lastly, we construct a dictionary for each category of topics based on the key words identified by BERTopics.[7] We use the dictionary to code which categories of topics were mentioned in each of the responses. We treat the categories

---

[7] Note that three categories appear in both the economic and cultural dimensions: welfare services, immigration, and environment. These categories were generated independently for each dimension and therefore their dictionaries also differ.

**Table 3** Example responses for topics in cultural dimension

| Category | Example |
|---|---|
| **Immigration** | "Most parties disagree with immigration and all the foreigners in the country" |
| | "I think immigration is a very contensious [sic] subject that all parties have a different views on" |
| **Integration** | "Black Pete, keep Christian standards. no Islamization, but freedom of religion policy and not imposition" |
| | "Intolerance of cultural others, violation of democracy" |
| **Traditional morality** | "Catholic Church, the imposition of Catholic dogma on people such as atheists, PiS's representation of dictatorial power, the politicization of the courts" |
| | "Things that the parties disagree on are abortion and immigration" |
| **Welfare services** | "Combating poverty in old age, higher standard rates for recipients of basic benefits" |
| | "Hartz 4, social benefits and pension" |
| **Environment** | "Immigration & climate or environmental protection" |
| | "Immigration is an important issue on which tolerances vary widely among the various parties. The tolerance levels vary greatly between the different parties. Equal rights and, above all, environmental protection and nature conservation are also important" |

**Table 4** Example responses for topics in economic dimension

| Category | Example |
| --- | --- |
| Inequality | *"One of the things can be the tax on how high or low it should be and how it can affect our everyday life"* |
| | *"inequality; conservative right wing parties don't address this issue. actually their policies make it worse"* |
| Welfare services | *"fair tax distribution. support for the economically vulnerable, healthcare and education for all"* |
| | *"Immigration policy and the budget for schools, care and health care differ between the parties"* |
| Labor market | *"Unemployment, evictions, inter-party corruption, unemployment and job insecurity"* |
| | *"they should help the people more the people extend a hand and help people job-wise, give jobs to young people even without experience, we need to Lower taxes, rents, gasoline, light gas utilities, because today you don't live anymore, you need freedom"* |
| Immigration | *"the key economic issues are immigration and letting illegal immigrants in and also healthcare is a big problem"* |
| | *"we have a terrible problem with illegals we cannot take care of our own people and they want to take on more and set them up with free housing, healthcare etc."* |
| Environment | *"The climate agreement which will cost trillions and hardly deliver anything. A tesla gets a subsidy; where does that power come from? Coal and lignite"* |
| | *"the environment I find the biggest economic problem in politics"* |

**Table 5** Summary of respondents' replies

|  | Cultural dimension | Economic dimension |
|---|---|---|
| N | 3,549 | 3,659 |
| Average character length | 29.08 | 27.78 |
| Average # of words | 4.61 | 4.54 |
| At least one topic mentioned | 1,838 | 1,900 |
| Average # of topics | 0.72 | 0.78 |
| Don't know (in %) | 16.34 | 15.92 |

**Note:** This table provides descriptive summary of open-ended responses in the cultural and economic dimensions.

of topics as nonmutually exclusive: that is, if a response mentioned both "immigrants" and "green," it was coded as both "immigration" and "environment." As shown in Table 5, respondents mentioned on average 0.78 (0.72) topics in their reply to the economic (cultural) dimension, while 15.92% (16.34%) of all respondents indicated they did not know how to answer the question. The full dictionary is presented in the appendix in Tables C.2 and C.1. We also identified words that were used when respondents indicated to not know how to respond to the question.

While about half of the responses fall into one of the coded topics, 47% of responses do not mention any of the topics we coded. This category of "non-responses" is heterogeneous: It includes survey participants who simply answered "don't know" or "no idea," as well as those who argued that there is no difference between parties. Other respondents gave nonsensical answers (e.g., "pizza, dancing, singing"). Of course, other topics that we did not code were mentioned as well. For instance, some responses mentioned the pandemic, civil rights, or trade. Another group of responses consists of country-specific concerns such as Brexit in the UK or the Catalan independence movement in Spain. In the analyses in Section 4, we include all of these responses.

## 3.3 Do Not Know

As already mentioned, 15.9% of respondents indicated they do not know what are the economic issues on which parties disagree, while 16.3% respondent said the same with regard to cultural disagreements. These "don't know" responses are not distributed randomly, as shown in Table 6. Female respondents and those with lower levels of education and income were more likely to indicate they do not know how to define the two dimensions. It is only for the economic

**Table 6** Regression of indicating "don't know" on individual characteristics for both conditions

| | Don't know | |
|---|---|---|
| | Cultural dimension | Economic dimension |
| (Intercept) | 0.077** | 0.090*** |
| | (0.027) | (0.027) |
| Age | −0.014* | −0.033*** |
| | (0.006) | (0.006) |
| Age squared | 0.010+ | 0.009 |
| | (0.006) | (0.006) |
| Male | −0.064*** | −0.059*** |
| | (0.012) | (0.012) |
| Medium education | 0.034* | 0.027* |
| | (0.014) | (0.013) |
| Low education | 0.101*** | 0.132*** |
| | (0.020) | (0.019) |
| No education | 0.242*** | 0.195*** |
| | (0.034) | (0.035) |
| Rural | −0.007 | 0.027* |
| | (0.014) | (0.014) |
| Medium HH inc | 0.011 | −0.032 |
| | (0.021) | (0.020) |
| Low HH inc | 0.050** | 0.014 |
| | (0.019) | (0.019) |
| HH inc missing | 0.125*** | 0.074** |
| | (0.026) | (0.025) |
| Num.Obs. | 3471 | 3594 |
| R2 | 0.058 | 0.065 |
| R2 Adj. | 0.053 | 0.060 |
| Country-<br>  FE included | yes | yes |

**Note:** $+p < 0.1$, $*p < 0.05$, $**p < 0.01$, $***p < 0.001$. Coefficients estimated based on linear probability models. For education and income levels, the reference categories are "High education," and "High income." The dependent variable "Don't know" is a dummy variable equal to 1 if respondents indicated to not know about the reasons for party disagreement. Age variables are standardized.

dimension that rural respondents were more likely to opt for "don't know." These patterns are not entirely surprising, as lower income and lower levels of education are both associated with lower levels of political interest and different forms of political participation (Oser et al., 2013).

## 3.4 Intersection of Topics

In their open-ended answers to the economic and cultural issue prompts, disproportionate numbers of respondents reference the issue areas discussed in the prompts without name-checking any other issue areas, which is evidence that the prompts cued respondents' issue attention (see Figure A.1 in the appendix). Many respondents, however, discuss more than one topic. We examine how respondents link topics in their open-ended responses by visualizing associations between the appearance of topics in Figure 1. For the economic dimension, we see that labor markets, inequality, and welfare services are commonly discussed together. Interestingly, Figure 1 shows that about 27% of all responses mentioning immigration also include references to welfare services. This finding previews our discussion in Section 4.4 of how concerns over immigration and welfare services are intertwined in respondents' worldviews.

Turning to the cultural dimension, we find that immigration was the most common additional topic among those who mentioned welfare services – in line with our findings from analyses of the open-ended responses regarding the economic dimension. Our findings also indicate that immigration was the topic most often discussed jointly with all other topics. Over 40% of all responses mentioning the environment also mentioned immigration suggesting a linkage in respondents' minds between the two "new politics" issues. Immigration itself is most often discussed next to the topic of integration, which is reasonable considering that the two topics are substantively closely related.

## 3.5 Summary: Empirical Strategy

In this section, we described our dataset, presented the tools we use to analyze it, and established the categories of topics we identified in the open-ended responses and examined how they intersect. For the sake of transparency and reproducibility, and since the text analysis of the open-ended questions requires the development of a coding scheme (Haaland et al., 2024, 16), we summarize these steps in Table 7. We now turn to analyze variation in responses to the open-ended questions along three levels of analysis: countries, individual-level demographics, and the left–right divide.

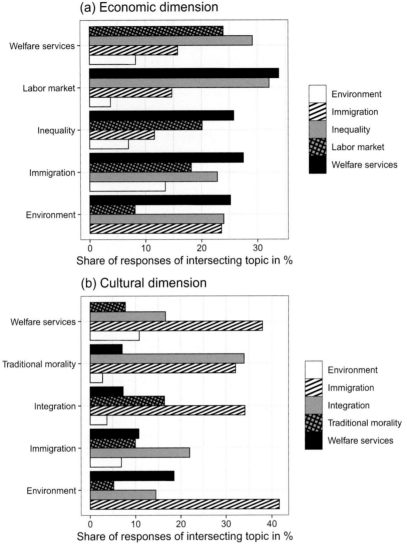

**Figure 1** Intersection of topics in open-ended responses
**Note**: This figure visualizes which topics were discussed in open-ended responses (colored bars) conditional on a given topic (topics on y-axis).

## 4 Results

Which issues do ordinary citizens associate with the economic and cultural dimensions of electoral politics? To answer this question, we begin by comparing responses to our two open-ended questions. We use keyness statistics to identify words that were most distinctive for respondents' definitions of each dimension (Zollinger, 2024). The results are presented in Figure 2.

**Table 7** Steps in preprocessing and empirical analysis

| Step | Description |
| --- | --- |
| **1. Translation** | We translated all open-ended responses into English using the DeepL API. We checked the accuracy of the translation in a subsample of replies |
| **2. Explorative topic modeling** | We used BERTopic to identify topics within the replies without predetermining number of topics (Figures B.1 and B.2 in the appendix) |
| **3. Classification of topics** | We classified the respective BERTopic topics into broader categories based on the evaluation of topic labels and word frequencies provided by BERTopic. We identified five broad categories of topics for each of the two dimensions |
| **4. Creation of dictionaries** | Based on key words provided for each topic by BERTopics, we created a dictionary for each of the categories of topics (Tables C.1 and C.2 in the appendix) |
| **5. Country-level analysis** | We examine variations across countries by calculating the share of respondents who mentioned each category of topics. Using a two-sided t-test, we determine whether one country's share of responses mentioning a category of topics deviates significantly from the combined share of all other countries (Tables 8 and 9) |
| **6. Demographic predictors** | We analyze which demographic variables predict mentioning a category (Tables 10 and 11) |
| **7. Variations across left–right** | We analyze which categories of topics predict left–right self-identification and partisanship (Tables 12 and 13) |

We find strong evidence that the public meaningfully distinguishes between the economic and cultural dimensions and associates specific policy issues with each of them. When asked to define economic and cultural disagreements in the political arena, ordinary citizens use distinct words that are in line with what we would expect based on existing work on this topic. Looking at the

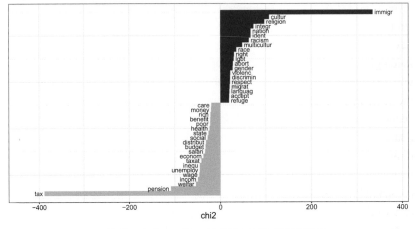

▪ Cultural dimension ▪ Economic dimension

**Figure 2** Keyness statistics by ideological dimension
**Note**: The figure shows terms mentioned with greatest relative frequency by respondents in the cultural dimension condition, relative to respondents describing the economic dimension. We apply stemming to combine words with identical word stems.

most distinctive word for each dimension, we find that respondents asked to elaborate on cultural issues mention "immigration" much more frequently than when asked about the economic dimension, while the reverse is true for "taxes."

This is not surprising, given that our questions mentioned these words as examples of economic and cultural issues on which parties may disagree. These keyness statistics thus first provide a basic test for our respondents' attention. Yet other words that were not mentioned in the prompt also clearly separate how ordinary citizens think about the content of the economic and cultural dimensions. Distinctive words for the cultural dimensions include "religion," "gender," "abortion," "lgbt," and "identity." In spite of the claim that the content of the second dimension has shifted to focus on national identity (Kriesi et al., 2008), the public clearly thinks about cultural issues also in terms of sexual identities, as we will discuss in length later on. Shifting to the economic dimension, the words "pensions," "inequality," "welfare," and "budget" are highly distinctive. Put differently, redistribution policies of taxing and spending, not pre-distribution (Diamond and Chwalisz, 2015), dominate how the public thinks about economic partisan disputes.

## 4.1 Country-Level Variations

To what degree do common understandings of the economic and cultural dimensions vary across countries? Scholars have examined this issue at the level of political elites and found that both dimensions are interpreted rather similarly across national borders. Specifically, the Chapel Hill Expert Survey, a commonly used dataset which provides experts' assessments of partisan ideological positions (Jolly et al., 2022), includes anchoring vignettes that allow scholars to investigate cross-national differences (and similarities) in the meanings of ideological dimensions. There is clear evidence that the economic dimension functions similarly across different European countries (Bakker et al., 2014). Furthermore, there is also evidence that the cultural dimension – which, as already discussed, likely has more heterogeneous meanings across time and space – similarly shows "a high degree of pan-European comparability" (Bakker et al., 2022). These findings pertain to political elites, and specifically parties; do they hold also when shifting to ordinary citizens?

To answer this question, we first analyze the share of responses that mentioned each of the categories of topics described in Tables 3 and 4, and the results for the cultural dimension are presented in Table 8. Percentages do not add to 100% since respondents can mention more than one topic in their response. Using a two-sided t-test, we determine whether one country's share of responses mentioning a category of topics deviates significantly from the combined share of all other countries. Grey shaded cells indicate that a country deviates from other countries' average ($p < 0.05$). More shaded cells in a column hint to a higher degree of cross-national variation for a given topic.

While immigration stands out as the most distinctive term defining the cultural dimension in our keyness statistics (Figure 2), its prevalence varies cross-nationally. This could be seen already from the fact that there are multiple shaded cells in the immigration column in Table 8. Around 30% of all responses to the question about the cultural dimension mentioned immigration, but the range is quite substantive: from around 40% of survey respondents in Germany, Greece, and Italy to just 11% in Poland. Closely related to immigration is the topic of integration, which is the second in prevalence. Integration is mentioned in around 19% of all responses ranging from almost 25% in the United States to closer to 13% in Italy.

Remaining topics – traditional morality, welfare services, and the environment – are mentioned less frequently than immigration and integration. With regard to traditional morality, Poland again stands out: while the overall average of responses mentioning traditional morality is less than 10%, in Poland it is 26%. Next in line for the share of responses mentioning traditional morality are Spain and the United States. The prominence of traditional morality in Poland, and to a lesser degree Spain and the United States, likely reflects the role of religion in these countries' politics and trajectories of nation-building.

**Table 8** Share of responses mentioning topic by country (cultural dimension)

| Country | Integration | Immigration | Traditional morality | Welfare services | Environment |
|---|---|---|---|---|---|
| France | 30.91% | 17.27% | 7.27% | 4.55% | 6.06% |
| Germany | 40.17% | 19.36% | 5.2% | 12.72% | 16.76% |
| Greece | 41.03% | 20% | 6.41% | 9.23% | 2.05% |
| Italy | 40.78% | 12.62% | 7.12% | 10.36% | 2.27% |
| Netherlands | 36.41% | 22.55% | 4.35% | 7.07% | 9.78% |
| Poland | 11.11% | 14.62% | 26.02% | 4.09% | 0.29% |
| Spain | 27.84% | 19.46% | 11.98% | 11.08% | 1.5% |
| Sweden | 32.29% | 20.86% | 6.86% | 8.57% | 3.71% |
| UK | 24.93% | 20.18% | 8.9% | 11.57% | 4.15% |
| US | 15.07% | 24.93% | 9.86% | 6.03% | 3.01% |
| Average | 30.08% | 19.33% | 9.33% | 8.5% | 4.98% |

**Note:** Percentages do not add up to 100% since topics were not mutually exclusive and respondents could mention more than one topic in their replies. Grey shaded cells indicate that a country's share deviates significantly ($p < 0.05$) from the other countries' average in a two-sided t-test.

While traditional morality is relatively common in descriptions of the cultural dimension in Poland and Spain, in both countries references to green policies are less than the overall sample average of 5%. In Poland, the green topic is practically nonexistent. Germany is an outlier, with closer to 17% mentioning issues related to the environment when asked about cultural partisan disputes.

Lastly, welfare services are mentioned in the context of the cultural dimension in 8.5% of the responses in the overall sample. It is more common in Germany, Spain, and the United Kingdom – and less so in Poland and France. Not surprisingly, welfare services are mentioned much more commonly in responses that describe the economic dimension, as we now turn to discuss.

Cross-national variations in respondents' understanding of the economic dimension are presented in Table 9. The two most common topics on average are inequality (23.5% of responses) and welfare services (20.8% of responses). References to the topic of inequality range from around 17% in Poland to almost 35% in Spain. Welfare services were mentioned most frequently in Sweden (29% of responses) and the least in Poland. Next, the labor market topic was mentioned in around 15% of responses. This topic is especially common

**Table 9** Share of responses mentioning topic by country
(economic dimension)

| Country | Inequality | Welfare services | Labor market | Immigration | Environment/ Energy |
|---|---|---|---|---|---|
| France | 18.02% | 19.77% | 9.88% | 14.53% | 4.07% |
| Germany | 23.01% | 27.73% | 8.26% | 17.99% | 28.02% |
| Greece | 26.67% | 25.19% | 26.42% | 7.65% | 0.99% |
| Italy | 24.08% | 13.87% | 33.51% | 18.85% | 1.57% |
| Netherlands | 21.53% | 20.11% | 9.07% | 15.86% | 17% |
| Poland | 16.85% | 11.41% | 3.26% | 0.54% | 1.63% |
| Spain | 34.49% | 22.03% | 23.48% | 5.22% | 1.45% |
| Sweden | 26.42% | 29.38% | 9.43% | 18.06% | 4.58% |
| UK | 19.88% | 22.94% | 8.56% | 8.26% | 8.26% |
| US | 23.61% | 16.11% | 12.5% | 12.5% | 3.33% |
| Average | 23.51% | 20.81% | 14.75% | 11.94% | 6.84% |

**Note:** Percentages do not add up to 100% since topics were not mutually exclusive and respondents could mention more than one topic in their replies. Grey shaded cells indicate that a country's share deviates significantly ($p < 0.05$) from the other countries' average in a two-sided t-test.

in countries that were strongly hit by the financial crisis: Spain, Greece, and Italy. This suggests that the legacies of the Euro crisis – more than ten years after its peak – still structure the mass-level understandings of partisan disputes over economic policies (Hutter and Kriesi, 2019).

While immigration is the most distinctive topic identifying the cultural dimension (Figure 2), it is also associated with economic issues and was mentioned in 12% of the responses to the question about economic partisan disputes (compared to references in 30% of all responses to the question about the cultural dimension). This is in line with Dancygier and Margalit (2020), whose analyses of partisan manifestos show that "discussion of cultural aspects [of immigration] does not surpass attention to economic concerns." We find that this finding holds not only for parties but also at the mass level. There are significant cross-national variations, as implied by the relatively large number of shaded cells. Immigration comes up in the context of the economic dimension more often in Italy, Sweden, and Germany but much less so in Spain and Greece, and it is virtually absent in Poland. As can be seen in Table 4, and as will be further discussed in Section 4.4, those who mentioned immigration in the context of the economic dimension often raised concerns about pressures from immigrants on welfare services such as healthcare and housing.

Lastly, issues related to environmental policies and energy were mentioned in almost 7% of responses to the question about the economic dimension. While Green policies are commonly understood as part of the second, noneconomic dimension (Hooghe and Marks, 2018; Inglehart, 1984), this topic is in fact more common, on average, in our respondents' interpretations of the economic dimension. Again there are stark differences across the countries in our sample. Germany stands out for the high degree to which the economic dimension is interpreted through a green lens: About 28% of German responses relate to this topic when asked about the economic dimension (compared to 16% of German responses that mentioned it in the context of the cultural dimension). Germany is followed by the Netherlands, where 17% of responses mentioned this topic. In all other countries, references to the environment were mentioned in less than 10% of the responses. In Greece, Poland, Italy, and Spain, this topic is mentioned in less than 2% of responses.

### 4.1.1 Cross-National Variations and Partisan Issue Salience

There are multiple potential explanations for these cross-national variations, with one immediate prominent suspect being the salience of issues raised by parties in each of these countries. That is, we can expect that if parties emphasize a certain issue, we would find this issue more frequently in the open-ended responses. However, we find little evidence to support this intuitive expectation.

To examine this issue, we correlate the prevalence of issues mentioned in the open-ended responses with issue salience items from the Chapel Hill Expert Survey (CHES). The CHES provides information on parties' positions and salience of issues based on expert codings, which have been validated extensively in previous research (Bakker et al., 2015; Jolly et al., 2022). The 2019 CHES wave includes data on the relative salience of immigration, environment, multiculturalism (closest to *integration* in our topic classification), and redistribution (closest to *inequality*) in parties' public stance. To generate a measure of issue salience for each of these topics in each country, we average across all party salience values and weight on each party's vote share. Then, in Figure 3, we plot these country averages against the respective country shares presented in Tables 8 and 9. The figure shows that issue salience and the share of respondents are, if at all, only weakly correlated. This suggests that people's interpretations of the main dimensions structuring the party system are not merely an automatic reflection of partisan issue salience at the aggregate country-level – at least not according to the salience measure provided by CHES.

This (non-)finding aligns with previous work on the connection (or lack thereof) between party system issue salience and the public's issue attention.

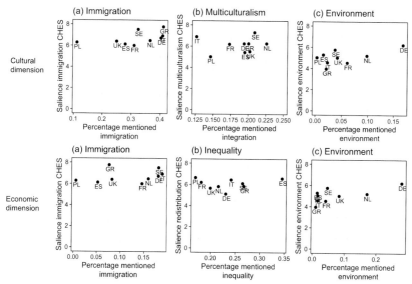

**Figure 3** CHES issue salience and shares of respondent mentioning issue
**Note**: This figure plots for each country the salience of a given issue based on expert codings in the CHES against the share of respondents in our survey discussing the respective issue. The top (bottom) row indicates the shares of respondents asked about the cultural (economic) dimension.

In a comprehensive comparative study of this topic, covering thirteen western European countries for a time period of half a century, Seeberg and Adams (2024) "uncover only weak and inconsistent evidence that the aggregate level of attention to an issue area among the political parties in the system … predicts subsequent shifts in the mass public's issue attention." This, however, does not suggest lack of association between the issues parties and elected politicians emphasize and their supporters' issue attention – something to which we return later, in our analyses of variations in the open-ended responses across party families.

To summarize this section, the analyses in Tables 8 and 9 suggest that common understandings of the economic and cultural dimensions differ across countries. While previous work examined cross-nationally both differences (Benoit and Laver, 2006) as well as similarities (Bakker et al., 2022, 2014) in the dimensionality of the electoral space, we demonstrate that *voters'* interpretation of the two dimensions differ to a certain degree across countries. Specifically, we find variations in the degree to which the "new right" issue of immigration and "new left" issue of environmental policies were absorbed into the economic and cultural dimensions (Kitschelt and Hellemans, 1990; Kriesi et al., 2008). While the rise in prominence of the cultural dimension has been documented across countries (Hall, 2020; Hall et al., 2023; Norris and Inglehart, 2019; Sides et al., 2022), its meaning has not been homogenized: in some countries it remains more strongly associated with gender roles and family structures, while in others it is defined first and foremost by questions of immigration and national identity. The economic dimension, in turn, is infused with topics that are commonly considered identity-related such as immigration and and green policies. These findings should encourage scholars to consider how ordinary citizens reason about immigration, the environment, and even welfare policies in ways that combine economic and cultural interpretations, as we will discuss in the last part of the Results section.

## 4.2 Variations Across Demographic Characteristics

Next, we turn to examine differences in the meanings attributed to the two dimensions across socio-demographic variables, and again we begin with the cultural dimension. Using linear probability models, we regress a set of binary variables, defined as whether respondents mentioned one of our categories of topics, on a vector of demographic variables: age (standardized), gender, education, rural–urban environment, and household income. We include a quadratic term for age to account for the possibility of a nonlinear relationship between age groups and the topic mentioned in the open-ended responses. The results are presented in Table 10, where we add country-fixed effects to capture within-country variations. We also control for the number of topics mentioned, as certain demographic groups (e.g., older people) appear to be more likely to mention more than one topic. Not controlling for the number of topics would therefore confound coefficients for these variables (e.g., age). We include a dummy variable for those respondents who preferred not to report their household income (HH inc missing).

There are several null results: income, gender, and rural–urban environment are not strongly associated with respondents' interpretations of the cultural dimension. This is not the case with regard to age: older and younger people have different issues in mind when asked about cultural ideological disagreements. Older people are more likely to mention issues related to immigration and less likely to point at topics related to traditional morality. A one standard deviation ($SD = 12.8$) increase in age is associated with a 3% (1.2%) increase (decrease) in the likelihood of mentioning immigration (traditional morality), all else equal.

To further explore age-based differences in understandings of the cultural dimension, we turn to keyness statistics to identify the most distinctive words for younger and older respondents. The results, presented in Figure 4,

**Table 10** Regression of mentioned topics on individual characteristics (cultural dimension)

|  | Immigration | Integration | Traditional morality | Welfare services | Environment |
|---|---|---|---|---|---|
| (Intercept) | 0.286*** | 0.102*** | 0.013 | 0.077*** | 0.125*** |
|  | (0.031) | (0.027) | (0.020) | (0.020) | (0.016) |
| Age | 0.030*** | 0.002 | −0.012* | 0.009* | −0.005 |
|  | (0.007) | (0.006) | (0.005) | (0.005) | (0.004) |
| Age squared | 0.003 | −0.006 | −0.002 | −0.006 | −0.001 |
|  | (0.007) | (0.006) | (0.004) | (0.005) | (0.004) |
| Male | −0.005 | 0.014 | −0.014 | 0.005 | 0.008 |
|  | (0.014) | (0.012) | (0.009) | (0.009) | (0.007) |
| Medium education | −0.016 | −0.011 | −0.021* | 0.002 | −0.008 |
|  | (0.016) | (0.014) | (0.010) | (0.010) | (0.008) |
| Low education | −0.049* | −0.043* | −0.016 | 0.003 | −0.011 |
|  | (0.022) | (0.019) | (0.014) | (0.014) | (0.011) |
| No education | −0.148*** | −0.060+ | −0.040 | −0.010 | −0.018 |
|  | (0.038) | (0.033) | (0.025) | (0.025) | (0.019) |
| Rural | 0.004 | −0.023+ | −0.001 | 0.011 | 0.007 |
|  | (0.016) | (0.014) | (0.010) | (0.010) | (0.008) |
| Medium HH inc | 0.053* | −0.002 | −0.008 | −0.006 | 0.009 |
|  | (0.024) | (0.021) | (0.015) | (0.016) | (0.012) |
| Low HH inc | 0.012 | −0.005 | −0.003 | −0.028* | 0.012 |
|  | (0.021) | (0.018) | (0.014) | (0.014) | (0.011) |
| HH inc missing | −0.030 | 0.001 | −0.018 | −0.026 | 0.004 |
|  | (0.029) | (0.026) | (0.019) | (0.019) | (0.015) |
| Two topics | 0.475*** | 0.468*** | 0.251*** | 0.223*** | 0.123*** |
|  | (0.020) | (0.017) | (0.013) | (0.013) | (0.010) |
| Three or more topics | 0.703*** | 0.592*** | 0.564*** | 0.414*** | 0.315*** |
|  | (0.044) | (0.038) | (0.028) | (0.029) | (0.022) |

**Table 10**  (Cont.)

|            | Immigration | Integration | Traditional morality | Welfare services | Environment |
|------------|-------------|-------------|----------------------|------------------|-------------|
| Num.Obs.   | 3,471       | 3,471       | 3,471                | 3,471            | 3,471       |
| R2         | 0.243       | 0.225       | 0.214                | 0.137            | 0.131       |
| R2 Adj.    | 0.238       | 0.221       | 0.209                | 0.132            | 0.126       |
| Country-FE included | yes | yes      | yes                  | yes              | yes         |

**Note:** $+p < 0.1$, $*p < 0.05$, $**p < 0.01$, $***p < 0.001$. Coefficients estimated based on linear probability models. For education and income levels, and number of topics mentioned, the reference categories are "High education," "High income," and "1 or none of the topics mentioned." Age variables are standardized.

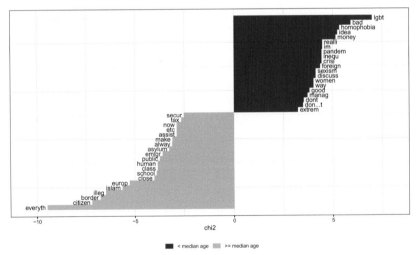

**Figure 4** Keyness for young vs. old respondents in the cultural dimension
**Note**: This figure shows terms mentioned with greatest relative frequency by young vs. old respondents (median split) among respondents cultural dimension condition.

underscore the point that older people think about the cultural dimension in terms of national identity: Among the most distinctive words for respondents above the median age are "borders," "illegal(s)," "asylum," and "Islam." In contrast, respondents below the median age (which is forty in our sample) define the cultural dimension in terms of gender and sexual identities: Among the most distinctive words we find "lgbt," "homophobia," and "sexism."

**Table 11** Regression of mentioned topics on individual characteristics (economic dimension)

| | Inequality | Welfare services | Labor market | Immigration | Environment/ energy |
|---|---|---|---|---|---|
| (Intercept) | 0.104*** | 0.112*** | −0.044+ | 0.081*** | 0.229*** |
| | (0.029) | (0.026) | (0.023) | (0.023) | (0.018) |
| Age | −0.002 | 0.016** | 0.015** | 0.007 | 0.000 |
| | (0.006) | (0.006) | (0.005) | (0.005) | (0.004) |
| Age squared | 0.014* | −0.007 | −0.019*** | 0.003 | 0.002 |
| | (0.007) | (0.006) | (0.005) | (0.005) | (0.004) |
| Male | 0.004 | −0.013 | 0.014 | 0.014 | 0.004 |
| | (0.013) | (0.012) | (0.010) | (0.010) | (0.008) |
| Low education | −0.075*** | −0.021 | 0.002 | −0.006 | −0.010 |
| | (0.021) | (0.019) | (0.016) | (0.016) | (0.012) |
| Medium education | −0.022 | −0.009 | 0.007 | 0.011 | 0.000 |
| | (0.015) | (0.013) | (0.011) | (0.011) | (0.009) |
| No education | −0.114** | −0.070* | 0.020 | −0.049+ | 0.019 |
| | (0.038) | (0.034) | (0.030) | (0.029) | (0.023) |
| Rural | −0.013 | 0.008 | −0.016 | 0.006 | 0.008 |
| | (0.015) | (0.013) | (0.012) | (0.011) | (0.009) |
| Low HH inc | 0.017 | 0.038* | −0.008 | −0.029+ | −0.006 |
| | (0.020) | (0.018) | (0.016) | (0.015) | (0.012) |
| Medium HH inc | 0.047* | 0.010 | −0.006 | 0.020 | 0.002 |
| | (0.022) | (0.020) | (0.017) | (0.017) | (0.013) |
| HH inc missing | 0.040 | −0.011 | −0.022 | −0.015 | 0.014 |
| | (0.027) | (0.025) | (0.022) | (0.021) | (0.017) |
| Two topics | 0.386*** | 0.452*** | 0.366*** | 0.239*** | 0.112*** |
| | (0.018) | (0.016) | (0.014) | (0.013) | (0.011) |
| Three or more topics | 0.602*** | 0.692*** | 0.537*** | 0.470*** | 0.285*** |
| | (0.032) | (0.029) | (0.025) | (0.025) | (0.019) |
| Num.Obs. | 3,594 | 3,594 | 3,594 | 3,594 | 3,594 |
| R2 | 0.194 | 0.283 | 0.291 | 0.183 | 0.176 |
| R2 Adj. | 0.189 | 0.279 | 0.287 | 0.178 | 0.171 |
| Country-FE included | yes | yes | yes | yes | yes |

**Note:** $+p < 0.1$, $*p < 0.05$, $**p < 0.01$, $***p < 0.001$. Coefficients estimated based on linear probability models. For education and income levels, and number of topics mentioned, the reference categories are "High education," "High income," and "1 or none of the topics mentioned." Age variables are standardized.

There are also individual-level differences in respondents' understanding of the economic dimension (see Table 11). Again, we use linear probability models to regress our dependent variables (topics mentioned in open-ended responses) on the same demographic variables. Again, gender and rural–urban environment fail to predict the topic mentioned. Inequality is more likely to be mentioned by those with higher levels of education compared to those with lower levers of education.

As with the cultural dimension, our analyses uncover age-based differences in people's understanding of the economic dimension. With regard to inequality, the relationship is nonlinear – in line with recent work that shows nonlinear relationship between economic preferences and age (Aspide et al., 2023). The positive coefficient for the squared age variable indicates that mentioning inequality is more common among younger and older respondents, and less common in the medium age groups. The reverse is true when examining the probability of mentioning the labor market topic: the negative coefficient for squared age signals that this increase is not linear but decreases for the oldest age groups in our sample. One possible reason for this nonlinear relationship could be the lower labor market participation among very young and older respondents. Lastly, older respondents were more likely to mention welfare services.

To summarize this section, there are several null findings worth emphasizing: While there are reasons to expect gender and rural–urban environment to be associated with specific interpretations of the economic and cultural dimensions, our analyses failed to find such associations. That being said, our results do provide further evidence for the significance of the age divide in Western politics (Caughey et al., 2019; Lauterbach and De Vries, 2020) – not only in structuring people's cultural and economic preferences on specific policy issues (Norris and Inglehart, 2019; O'Grady, 2023) or in the importance they are expected to attach to cultural compared to economic issues (Mitteregger, 2024) but also in the basic understanding of the content of the two dimensions.

## 4.3 Variations Across the Left–Right Divide and Party Support

In the analyses in Section 4.2 we examined how demographic characteristics predict different understandings of the cultural and economic dimensions. We now turn to examine how different meanings ascribed to these dimensions are associated with left–right self-identification and party affiliation. Thus, the categories of topics defining the two dimensions shift from dependent to independent variables and our dependent variable is now an eleven-point scale of left–right self-identification, which strongly correlates with vote choice

(Dalton, 2010). We also analyze as the dependent variable respondents' in-party, classified into party families based on data from the Comparative Manifesto Project (Volkens et al., 2017). We coded the party that individuals indicated they felt closest to as respondents' in-party. If an individual did not indicate any party, they were asked if there was a party that they felt somewhat close to, which was then used as in-party. If no party was indicated, we used individuals' vote choice in the past election. Our models are rather demanding, since in addition to the understandings of the cultural and economic dimension, we account also for individual-level variables and country-level fixed effects.

We begin with the cultural dimension and the results are presented in Table 12. The demographic variables perform as expected in predicting in-party identification: older people are more likely to affiliate with Conservative and radical right parties, respondents with lower education are less likely to support Liberal parties, and rural voters are more likely to support radical right parties. This lends face validity to our analyses of partisan identities.

Do people's understandings of the cultural dimension relate to their left–right position and in-party choice, even after we account for these demographic variables? Our results suggest that is indeed the case. Defining the cultural dimension in terms of traditional morality and integration is predictive of self-identifying as leftist. The coefficient for relating to traditional morality is substantial, moving the eleven-point left–right scale, all else equal, by more than 0.5 points to the left. In comparison, the respective coefficient for the gender dummy (0.314) is about 40% weaker. That is, associating the cultural dimension with issues of gender roles is more strongly predictive of left-wing support than respondents' gender – a variable that has been shown to strongly and consistently predict left–right self-identification (Dassonneville, 2021).

Shifting from left–right self-identification to in-parties, we see that defining the cultural dimension in terms of immigration is predictive of supporting radical right and conservative parties. In contrast, associating the cultural dimension with integration is predictive of support for green parties, albeit the relationship is substantively smaller than that between immigration and the aforementioned parties on the right.[8] As can be expected, interpreting the cultural dimension in terms of the environment is predictive of support for green parties. And mentioning issues related to welfare services is associated with support for Christian Democratic parties. Thus, the meaning of the cultural dimension serves as a reliable predictor of people's ideological and partisan identities.

---

[8] Results remain very similar when we use vote choice instead of in-parties as dependent variable (see Table D.1 in the appendix).

**Table 12** Predicting party affiliation with mentioned topics (cultural dimension)

| | Left–right scale | Ecological | Left | Social-Dem. | Liberal | Christian-Dem. | Conservative | Nationalist |
|---|---|---|---|---|---|---|---|---|
| (Intercept) | 4.796*** | 0.153*** | 0.104*** | 0.162*** | 0.146*** | 0.239*** | 0.012 | 0.010 |
| | (0.211) | (0.015) | (0.022) | (0.029) | (0.021) | (0.018) | (0.027) | (0.025) |
| Immigration | 0.072 | 0.018* | 0.025* | −0.017 | 0.010 | −0.013 | 0.036* | 0.050*** |
| | (0.121) | (0.009) | (0.012) | (0.017) | (0.012) | (0.010) | (0.015) | (0.014) |
| Tradition/morality | −0.532** | −0.003 | 0.014 | 0.026 | 0.004 | 0.000 | −0.007 | −0.008 |
| | (0.185) | (0.013) | (0.019) | (0.026) | (0.019) | (0.016) | (0.023) | (0.022) |
| Environment | −0.037 | 0.058*** | −0.010 | 0.026 | 0.058* | 0.000 | −0.037 | −0.005 |
| | (0.232) | (0.016) | (0.024) | (0.032) | (0.024) | (0.019) | (0.029) | (0.028) |
| Welfare services | −0.055 | −0.004 | 0.021 | 0.021 | 0.025 | 0.034* | −0.028 | 0.019 |
| | (0.186) | (0.013) | (0.019) | (0.026) | (0.019) | (0.016) | (0.024) | (0.022) |
| Integration | −0.345* | 0.022* | 0.012 | 0.035+ | 0.006 | 0.003 | −0.035* | 0.025 |
| | (0.142) | (0.010) | (0.015) | (0.020) | (0.014) | (0.012) | (0.018) | (0.017) |
| Age | 0.036 | −0.008* | 0.007 | 0.003 | 0.001 | 0.008* | 0.033*** | 0.011* |
| | (0.046) | (0.003) | (0.005) | (0.006) | (0.005) | (0.004) | (0.006) | (0.005) |
| Age squared | −0.057 | 0.006+ | 0.002 | −0.019** | 0.003 | 0.000 | 0.003 | −0.002 |
| | (0.045) | (0.003) | (0.005) | (0.006) | (0.005) | (0.004) | (0.006) | (0.005) |
| Male | 0.314*** | −0.017** | 0.005 | −0.002 | 0.013 | −0.005 | 0.013 | 0.042*** |
| | (0.089) | (0.006) | (0.009) | (0.012) | (0.009) | (0.007) | (0.011) | (0.011) |
| Low education | 0.102 | −0.031** | −0.012 | −0.018 | −0.045** | −0.013 | 0.018 | 0.023 |
| | (0.144) | (0.010) | (0.015) | (0.020) | (0.015) | (0.012) | (0.018) | (0.017) |

| | (1) | (2) | (3) | (4) | (5) | (6) | (7) | (8) |
|---|---|---|---|---|---|---|---|---|
| Medium education | −0.095 | −0.004 | −0.022* | 0.004 | −0.048*** | −0.006 | −0.005 | 0.053*** |
| | (0.102) | (0.007) | (0.010) | (0.014) | (0.010) | (0.009) | (0.013) | (0.012) |
| No education | 0.168 | −0.044* | −0.007 | −0.006 | −0.053* | −0.022 | −0.014 | 0.004 |
| | (0.250) | (0.018) | (0.026) | (0.035) | (0.025) | (0.021) | (0.032) | (0.030) |
| Rural | 0.061 | −0.002 | 0.014 | −0.048*** | −0.007 | −0.013 | 0.006 | 0.028* |
| | (0.101) | (0.007) | (0.010) | (0.014) | (0.010) | (0.008) | (0.013) | (0.012) |
| Low HH inc | −0.398** | 0.019+ | 0.020 | −0.028 | −0.041** | −0.032** | −0.037* | 0.004 |
| | (0.138) | (0.010) | (0.014) | (0.019) | (0.014) | (0.012) | (0.017) | (0.016) |
| Medium HH inc | −0.348* | 0.010 | 0.006 | −0.020 | −0.035* | −0.006 | −0.029 | 0.010 |
| | (0.155) | (0.011) | (0.016) | (0.022) | (0.016) | (0.013) | (0.020) | (0.019) |
| HH inc missing | −0.613** | 0.017 | −0.005 | −0.075** | −0.057** | −0.050** | −0.062* | −0.029 |
| | (0.191) | (0.014) | (0.020) | (0.027) | (0.019) | (0.016) | (0.024) | (0.023) |
| Two topics | −0.224 | −0.021 | 0.012 | 0.003 | −0.031 | −0.019 | 0.013 | −0.044+ |
| | (0.202) | (0.014) | (0.021) | (0.028) | (0.021) | (0.017) | (0.026) | (0.024) |
| Three or more topics | 0.015 | −0.039 | 0.019 | −0.068 | −0.083* | 0.029 | 0.069 | −0.054 |
| | (0.393) | (0.028) | (0.041) | (0.055) | (0.040) | (0.033) | (0.050) | (0.047) |
| Num. Obs. | 3,471 | 3,471 | 3,471 | 3,471 | 3,471 | 3,471 | 3,471 | 3,471 |
| R2 | 0.045 | 0.079 | 0.092 | 0.115 | 0.122 | 0.192 | 0.120 | 0.069 |
| R2 Adj. | 0.038 | 0.073 | 0.085 | 0.109 | 0.116 | 0.186 | 0.113 | 0.062 |
| Country-FE included | yes | yes | yes | yes | yes | yes | yes | yes |

**Note:** $+p < 0.1$, $*p < 0.05$, $**p < 0.01$, $***p < 0.001$. Coefficients estimated based on OLS regression in column 1 and linear probability models in columns 2–8. For topics, education and income levels, and number of topics mentioned, the reference categories are "none of the defined topic mentioned," "High education," "High income," and "1 or none of the topics mentioned." Age variables are standardized.

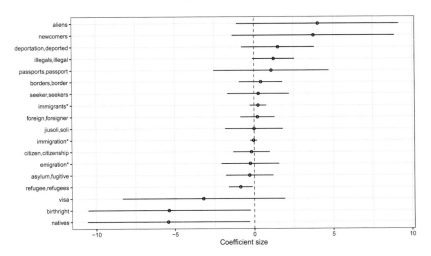

**Figure 5** Prediction of left–right scale based on words

**Note**: Shows regression coefficient for each word or group of words when regressing left–right scale on dummy for respective words. We also include country-fixed effects in the regression models. Words marked with * are bundling several words, mostly due to different typing of the same word. Horizontal lines indicate 95% confidence intervals.

Surprisingly, mentioning immigration when asked about the cultural dimension is also positively correlated with support for green and left parties, although the corresponding estimate is rather small. To explore this counterintuitive finding further, we use our dictionary for the immigration topic in the cultural dimension and correlate words with the left–right scale. In Figure 5, we show that there is a stark divide within our immigration dictionary: While words like *alien*, *newcomers*, *deportation*, or *illegals* are predominantly found on the political right, other words such as *refugees* or *natives* are predominantly mentioned on the political left. This heterogeneity within topics can resolve the puzzling correlation associated with the immigration topic in Table 12 – references to immigration across different parties are made through references to different concerns and policies.

Lastly, we examine how different interpretations of the economic dimension predict left–right self-identification and partisanship. The results are presented in Table 13. We find strong differences across the left–right divide: defining the economic dimension in terms of immigration is strongly associated with right-wing support, while references to inequality and the environment are predictive of left-wing support. Again, it is instructive to compare these coefficients with the dummy for male respondents. The coefficient for our immigration dummy is sizeable, moving the eleven-point left–right scale by more than 0.4 points to the right. In comparison, the respective coefficient

**Table 13** Predicting party affiliation with mentioned topics (economic dimension)

| | Left–right scale | Ecological | Left | Social-Dem. | Liberal | Christian-Dem. | Conservative | Nationalist |
|---|---|---|---|---|---|---|---|---|
| (Intercept) | 4.880*** | 0.199*** | 0.077*** | 0.140*** | 0.113*** | 0.216*** | 0.014 | 0.029 |
| | (0.209) | (0.016) | (0.020) | (0.029) | (0.021) | (0.018) | (0.027) | (0.024) |
| Welfare services | −0.282* | 0.018 | 0.019 | 0.043* | −0.006 | 0.000 | 0.010 | 0.019 |
| | (0.142) | (0.011) | (0.014) | (0.020) | (0.014) | (0.012) | (0.018) | (0.017) |
| Immigration | 0.420* | −0.005 | −0.022 | 0.006 | −0.021 | 0.014 | 0.010 | 0.142*** |
| | (0.165) | (0.013) | (0.016) | (0.023) | (0.016) | (0.014) | (0.021) | (0.019) |
| Inequality | −0.431*** | 0.023* | 0.034** | 0.045* | 0.014 | 0.002 | −0.006 | −0.002 |
| | (0.129) | (0.010) | (0.012) | (0.018) | (0.013) | (0.011) | (0.016) | (0.015) |
| Labor market | 0.140 | 0.016 | 0.013 | 0.038+ | −0.023 | 0.000 | 0.042* | −0.004 |
| | (0.163) | (0.013) | (0.016) | (0.023) | (0.016) | (0.014) | (0.021) | (0.019) |
| Environment/energy | −0.424* | 0.057*** | 0.012 | 0.044 | −0.012 | −0.026 | −0.013 | −0.019 |
| | (0.203) | (0.016) | (0.020) | (0.028) | (0.020) | (0.017) | (0.026) | (0.024) |
| Age | 0.089* | −0.003 | −0.006 | 0.007 | 0.001 | 0.002 | 0.030*** | 0.015** |
| | (0.044) | (0.003) | (0.004) | (0.006) | (0.004) | (0.004) | (0.006) | (0.005) |
| Age squared | −0.219*** | 0.003 | 0.003 | 0.001 | 0.001 | −0.002 | 0.010+ | −0.017** |
| | (0.045) | (0.003) | (0.004) | (0.006) | (0.004) | (0.004) | (0.006) | (0.005) |
| Male | 0.363*** | 0.001 | 0.010 | 0.010 | −0.010 | −0.006 | −0.014 | 0.064*** |
| | (0.087) | (0.007) | (0.008) | (0.012) | (0.009) | (0.007) | (0.011) | (0.010) |
| Low education | −0.055 | −0.015 | −0.010 | −0.046* | −0.049*** | −0.007 | −0.002 | 0.016 |
| | (0.141) | (0.011) | (0.014) | (0.020) | (0.014) | (0.012) | (0.018) | (0.017) |
| Medium education | 0.060 | −0.035*** | −0.002 | −0.035* | −0.025* | 0.001 | 0.005 | 0.046*** |
| | (0.099) | (0.008) | (0.010) | (0.014) | (0.010) | (0.008) | (0.013) | (0.012) |

**Table 13** (Cont.)

| | Left–right scale | Ecological | Left | Social-Dem. | Liberal | Christian-Dem. | Conservative | Nationalist |
|---|---|---|---|---|---|---|---|---|
| No education | 0.492+ | −0.045* | −0.001 | −0.060+ | −0.104*** | −0.011 | −0.023 | 0.013 |
| | (0.257) | (0.020) | (0.025) | (0.036) | (0.026) | (0.022) | (0.033) | (0.030) |
| Rural | 0.305** | −0.014+ | −0.019+ | −0.044** | 0.001 | 0.005 | 0.055*** | 0.013 |
| | (0.101) | (0.008) | (0.010) | (0.014) | (0.010) | (0.009) | (0.013) | (0.012) |
| Low HH inc | −0.371** | −0.008 | 0.008 | 0.021 | −0.030* | −0.010 | −0.042* | 0.024 |
| | (0.137) | (0.011) | (0.013) | (0.019) | (0.014) | (0.012) | (0.017) | (0.016) |
| Medium HH inc | −0.336* | −0.008 | −0.011 | 0.010 | −0.011 | 0.011 | −0.041* | 0.033+ |
| | (0.150) | (0.012) | (0.014) | (0.021) | (0.015) | (0.013) | (0.019) | (0.018) |
| HH inc missing | −0.319+ | −0.023 | −0.020 | −0.047+ | −0.039* | −0.010 | −0.075** | 0.019 |
| | (0.187) | (0.015) | (0.018) | (0.026) | (0.019) | (0.016) | (0.024) | (0.022) |
| Two topics | −0.023 | 0.001 | −0.012 | −0.058* | 0.021 | 0.009 | 0.008 | −0.035 |
| | (0.199) | (0.016) | (0.019) | (0.028) | (0.020) | (0.017) | (0.025) | (0.023) |
| Three or more topics | 0.223 | −0.026 | 0.027 | −0.116* | 0.026 | −0.033 | 0.004 | −0.006 |
| | (0.345) | (0.027) | (0.033) | (0.048) | (0.034) | (0.030) | (0.044) | (0.040) |
| Num. Obs. | 3594 | 3594 | 3594 | 3594 | 3594 | 3594 | 3594 | 3594 |
| R2 | 0.041 | 0.093 | 0.112 | 0.131 | 0.120 | 0.209 | 0.124 | 0.083 |
| R2 Adj. | 0.034 | 0.087 | 0.105 | 0.125 | 0.113 | 0.204 | 0.117 | 0.077 |
| Country-FE included | yes | yes | yes | yes | yes | yes | yes | yes |

**Note:** $+p < 0.1$, $*p < 0.05$, $**p < 0.01$, $***p < 0.001$. Coefficients estimated based on OLS regression in column 1 and linear probability models in columns 2–8. For topics, education and income levels, and number of topics mentioned, the reference categories are "none of the defined topic mentioned," "High education," "High income," and "1 or none of the topics mentioned." Age variables are standardized.

for male respondents (0.363) is about 14% weaker. The coefficient for our inequality dummy is about as large as that for immigration.

We can more closely examine this variation across the left–right divide by looking at in-party as the dependent variable. Defining the economic dimension in terms of immigration is strongly predictive of support for radical right parties. Interestingly, such an emphasis on immigration is not predictive of voting for other parties to the right of the center (Bale and Kaltwasser, 2021; Gidron, 2022). References to labor market policies are predictive of voting for conservative parties. On the other side of the left–right divide, we find that the topic of inequality is strongly predictive of support for green, far-left parties, and also social democrats. Defining the economic dimensions in terms of environmental policies is associated with support for green parties. Results remain substantively similar when looking at vote choice instead of partisan affiliation (see Table D.2 in the appendix), although when looking at voting the mentioning of green issues is no longer associated with voting for green parties. This may reflect the fact that green parties are no longer seen by some of their voters as single-issue parties, whose agenda is limited to environmental policies (Spoon and Williams, 2021).

To summarize this section, we find that the meaning attributed to the two-dimensional space varies across the left–right divide and based on people's partisan affiliation. That is, voters across the left–right divide (as well as across different party families) differ from one another not only in their positions on the economic and cultural dimensions but also in their understanding of what these dimensions stand for. This finding resonates with previous research on variations in issue attention. While they find no conclusive evidence of country-level linkage between what parties talk about and what the public cares about, Seeberg and Adams (2024) do find such a strong association at the party level. That is, there is an association between what parties prioritize and the issue their supporters find most important. This relationship, however, is dependent on parties' size and type: Klüver and Spoon (2016) provide evidence from across European polities that larger parties are more likely to prioritize the issue their voters care about. This cross-national evidence, based on the analyses of party platforms and public opinion surveys, is supported by country-specific case studies. Neundorf and Adams (2018) show that in both the UK and Germany, there is a reciprocal feedback loop in which citizens turn to parties that emphasize the issues they care about – while also adapting their issue attention to the topics emphasized by their preferred party. And in the United States, Barberá et al. (2019) provide evidence, based on the analysis of social media communication, that members of Congress emphasize issues prioritized by their voters – yet not necessarily those salient to the general public.

Our analyses say nothing about causal relationships: Our research design cannot speak to whether people's understanding of partisan disputes shapes their party support or vice versa. Our goal here is more limited: We identify systematic variations in how people make sense of the economic and cultural dimensions along the left–right divide and based on their partisan support.

### 4.4 Understanding Inequality at the Intersection of the Economic and Cultural Dimensions

A recurring theme in our analyses is that the boundaries between the economic and cultural dimensions are rather porous in people's minds. As already discussed, immigration and the environment were mentioned in survey responses that dealt with both dimensions. And references to welfare policies were also made when respondents were asked about cultural disputes that structure the electoral system. This calls for closer attention to the ways in which the two dimensions intersect.

To examine this issue, we turn to explore how the issue of *inequality* is discussed in the open-ended responses. Research on ordinary citizens' reasoning of contemporary politics highlights inequality as an issue which is interpreted through both economic and cultural lenses. Katherine Cramer's influential work on this exact topic delves into perceptions of inequalities across the rural–urban divide in the United States, particularly in Wisconsin (Cramer, 2016). In an article titled "Putting Inequality in Its Place," Cramer uses ethnographic methods to explore the ways in which rural identity is "imbued with perceptions of inequalities of power, differences in values, and also inequalities in resources" (p. 522; see also page 526). It is at this juncture of cultural values and material resources, or the cultural and the economic dimensions, that perceptions of inequality are shaped: rural residents feel not only discriminated against with regard to the distribution of material resources but also that their cultural way of life is looked down upon. As with ethnographic work, these insights are based on a single case study with limited claims to generalizability. Our cross-national dataset enables us to build on this research and to investigate whether and how references to inequality in the open-ended responses are shaped at the intersection of the two ideological dimensions.

In our empirical analyses of references to inequality, we distinguish between left-wing and right-wing supporters. This is because we have theoretical reasons to expect that if both left-wing and right-wing supporters mix economic and cultural perspectives when thinking about (in)equality, they will mix these perspectives differently. According to Norberto Bobbio, the core of the left–right distinction lies in its relationship to (in)equality, with the left being "more egalitarian" and the right "more inegalitarian" (Bobbio, 1996, 55–56).

Others, however, suggest that the difference between leftists and right-wing supporters is not with regard to how much they care about inequality, but rather which inequalities they care about. From this perspective, the right is "not, Bobbio notwithstanding, inegalitarian" but rather "differently egalitarian" (Noël and Thérien, 2008, 18).

To account for these differences in reasoning about inequality, we divide our sample of respondents into left-wing and right-wing supporters based on where they placed themselves on a scale ranging from 0 (far left) to 10 (far right). We classified respondents who positioned themselves between 0 and 4 as "left" and those who located themselves between 6 and 10 as "right."

We rely on manual coding to identify open-ended responses related to inequality. We classified responses as relating to inequality if they pertain to systemic differences between groups – or to different policies designed to address them, whether focused on taking from the advantaged group or on the receiving disadvantaged side (Cavaillé and Trump, 2015). Such manual classification allows us to detect responses that mention inequality in subtle ways.

Figure 6 presents the distribution of references to inequality after combining responses to questions on the economic and cultural dimensions. We find that left-wing identifiers are more likely to mention inequality in their responses compared to those on the right. Across all countries in our sample, 27% of left-wing supporters mentioned inequality, while only 23% of right-wing supporters did so. The size of the difference varies across countries, with smaller differences observed in Germany and larger differences observed in the United States. That being said, inequality was more frequently mentioned on the left in all countries in our sample.

More interesting for our purposes is not *how much* respondents mention inequality, but rather *how* they discuss the topic. To test this question, we zoom in on the responses that mention inequality and examine the most distinctive words used by respondents on the left and right. We start with the economic dimension, presenting the key words in Figure 7.

There are clear differences across the left–right divide. Left supporters' indicative words often refer to specific policy domains such as the minimum wage and health services. Those on the left also mentioned support for those who are in need and the importance of social insurance. Interestingly, issues of climate change were also mentioned in left-wing responses that dealt with economic inequalities[9] – even though, as already discussed, environmentalism is often associated with the second, cultural dimension.

---

[9] One left-wing respondent identified, e.g., "health, aid to people in need, ecological investment" as contested issues on the economic dimension. Another answer reads as follows: "jobs, sustainability, economic equality," directly addressing economic (in)equality and sustainability as environmental goal.

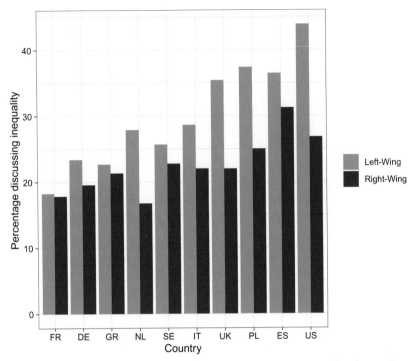

**Figure 6** Share of right-wing/left-wing respondents who mention inequality
**Note**: This figure shows for each country the share of right-wing/left-wing respondents discussing inequality in their open-ended responses. Respondents were classified in left- and right-wing supporters based on their position of a self-reported left–right scale (0–10). Observations between 0 and 4 as left, respondents who positioned themselves between 6 and 10 were coded as right wing.

We identify a different set of issues once we turn to responses provided by right-wing identifiers. As expected, we find references to taxation – as we would expect when focusing on inequality in the economic context. Yet immigration also stands out as a key issue, suggesting that citizens' pre-occupation with this topic is not limited to the cultural realm. References to immigration in the open-ended responses are often linked with concerns and critiques of the government, which is the most indicative word in the right-wing responses. Closer reading of the responses reveals that the government is often being portrayed as responsible for inequality by favoring groups that right-wing respondents see as undeserving.[10]

For instance, a German respondent pointed to welfare recipients as unde-serving of government assistance: "more and more taxes are useless if you are

---

[10] Since we use stemming, the word "government" appears in Figure 7 as "govern." and "immigration" as well as "immigrants" appear as "immigr."

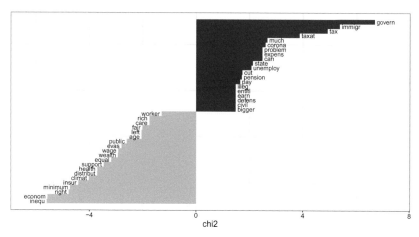

**Figure 7** Keyness statistics: Left-wing vs. Right-wing views on inequality in economic condition

**Note**: The figure shows terms mentioned with greatest relative frequency by right-wing respondents who discussed inequality in the economic dimension condition, relative to left-wing respondents. We apply stemming to combine words with identical word stems. Respondents were classified in left- and right-wing supporters based on their position of a self-reported left–right scale (0–10). Observations between 0 and 4 as left, respondents who positioned themselves between 6 and 10 were coded as right wing.

too stupid to save money by e.g. cutting Hartz 4 or kicking all illegals out of the country." A response from Poland directly linked this to unequal treatment of native-born citizens: "we have a terrible problem with illegals we cannot take care of our own people and they want to take on more and set them up with free housing, healthcare etc." Similarly, a Spanish respondent wrote: "spending on money for immigrants, those who do not feel Spanish and on associations that are worthless."

While immigrants are the primary group that right-wing respondents identify as undeserving recipients of government assistance, some responses targeted other groups such as young college students or LGBT people. In the words of one American respondent, "Democrats spend and give too much money out. Wanting to pay for college for instance. My generation and other generations managed just fine paying for their own degrees. Too many free handouts from the Democrats. Republicans take a more sensible approach and do not just start giving out money to any one." A Polish respondent wrote that "people get money for nothing, many housewives say that it is not necessary to go to work because what for if there is 500+ [Polish welfare program], they sit at home, they do not develop, they are not interested in anything, it creates a society warped, lazy, incapable of making decisions, besides it is LGBT, it is dangerous, it can not be cured."

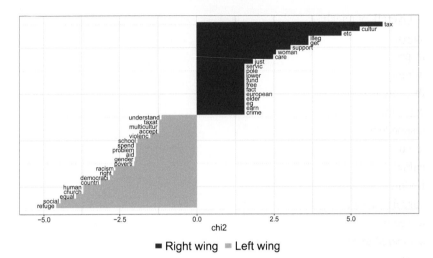

**Figure 8** Keyness statistics: left-wing vs. right-wing views on inequality in cultural condition

**Note**: The figure shows terms mentioned with greatest relative frequency by right-wing respondents who discussed inequality in the cultural dimension condition, relative to left-wing respondents. We apply stemming to combine words with identical word stems. Respondents were classified in left- and right-wing supporters based on their position of a self-reported left–right scale (0–10). Observations between 0 and 4 as left, respondents who positioned themselves between 6 and 10 were coded as right wing.

Turning to references of inequality mentioned by responses regarding the cultural dimension, we again find differences across the left–right divide and the results are presented in Figure 8. Left supporters who mentioned inequality often cited concerns about nativism and racism. In sharp contrast, right-wing supporters who mentioned inequalities when asked about the cultural dimension often referenced perceived preferential treatment of disadvantaged and culturally distinct groups. Indicative words such as "tax," "get," and "illegal" capture respondents' sense that taxpayer money is flowing to undeserving groups.

For instance, one respondent from Sweden mentioned in his response the following: "subsidies to new arrivals, 'free' health care dental care to illegal 'refugees'." Another response from the United States reflects on the same issue: "Immigrants getting free healthcare." In addition, right-wing respondents sometimes also vaguely referred to racial inequality and perceived privileges of certain groups: "people are saying the racism is against everyone but whites, I see it as everyone is now getting special privileges BUT the white people now because for some reason our government feels bad about something that happened [sic] sooo long ago and isn't anymore."

Overall, our analyses of references to inequality in the open-ended responses suggest that the boundaries between economic and cultural issues are blurring in people's minds. Again, the "new politics" issues of environmentalism and immigration challenge the distinction between the two dimensions. We find that this is particularly the case on the right. Whether they were asked about economic or cultural partisan disputes, references to inequalities by right-wing respondents often mentioned perceived economic discrimination compared to culturally distinct disadvantaged groups. This suggests that economic and cultural issues are closely intertwined in people's lived experiences. These findings echo those of Cramer (2016), who documented how right-wing rural consciousness serves as an economic-cultural lens through which people come to see themselves as economically discriminated against by the government compared to other groups such as urbanites and racial minorities.

The findings reported above also resonate with Sides et al. (2019) arguments about the ways in which Americans interpret economic developments through racialized lenses. In their analyses of the 2016 US elections, these authors argue that voters' concerns over economic conditions were inflected by cultural, and specifically racialized, grievances. Pushing against accounts that sought to identify whether Trump's supporters were motivated by economic or cultural concerns, Sides et al. (2019) proposed the notion of "racialized economics" as a theoretical middle ground: "Many people face clear economic challenges, and their concerns and anxieties are real. But when economic concerns are politically potent, the prism of identity is often present. This is 'racialized economics': the belief that undeserving groups are getting ahead while your group is left behind." This argument aligns with what we find in right-wing identifiers' references to inequality in the open-ended responses from across different European countries – suggesting that the interplay between economic and cultural factors is not unique to racial identities in the United States.

Closely related, in their analysis of reactions to growing inequality in the United States, Condon and Wichowsky (2020) consider how social comparisons shape political attitudes. They note that scholarly analyses of the 2016 US elections often sought to identify whether support for Trump was driven by economic or cultural concerns, yet when Americans "think about their own status, income and identity blend to paint the picture." Our analyses document this blending also outside the American context.

Our analyses cannot help us in uncovering the mechanisms that link economic and cultural perceptions of inequality. For instance, Rhodes-Purdy et al. (2023) argue that economic considerations come first and only then do cultural views follow. As these authors explain in their discussion of political discontent, "economic trauma, which spreads far and wide during economic crises, produces enduring arousal of negative emotions, namely anxiety and resentment" that often revolve around cultural conflicts over national and racial identities (p. 232). These authors view emotions as the transmission belt connecting economic grievances and cultural concerns, an approach that they label "affective political economy": as they explain, "economics are the roots, culture the branch, and emotions the trunk connecting the two" (p. 70). Our analyses uncover how closely economic and cultural perceptions are linked in people's minds but they do not delve into such mechanisms. Further work in this area could make a strong contribution to the field of public opinion research.

## 5 Conclusions

How does the theoretical construct of the two-dimensional ideological space – so commonly used in research on contemporary electoral politics – look like from voters' perspective? We have sought to answer this question through the analyses of open-ended survey questions collected in ten advanced democracies that differ in their political institutions, party system configurations, and economic arrangements. Our results uncover substantive variations across countries, age groups, the left–right divide and partisan support in how the public makes sense of the economic and cultural dimensions. Our findings also demonstrate how strongly economic and cultural issues are intertwined in people's reasoning about pressing political issues such as inequality.

### 5.1 Summarizing Our Key Findings

Our analyses uncover cross-national variations in the degree to which "new politics" issues of immigration and environmentalism have been absorbed into electoral competition. Both issues are raised by the public when asked about *both* the economic and cultural dimensions of electoral competition, although the degree to which they are mentioned varies significantly across countries. Specifically, we find that while environmentalism is often considered a cornerstone of the second, cultural dimension – is it also perceived by the public, and specifically in Germany, as associated with the economic dimension. This finding carries practical implications for how scholars approach the empirical operationalization of the two-dimensional framework. It complicates analyses that require scholars to decide in advance that each policy issue is associated with only a single ideological dimension.

Then, adding to research that has uncovered variations in the meaning of the ideological electoral space across countries (Benoit and Laver, 2006) – we find heterogeneous understandings of the economic and cultural dimensions even within the same country. We report a series of null results with regard to people's interpretation of the economic and cultural dimensions. Specifically, our analyses failed to detect meaningful correlations between the interpretation of these two dimensions and respondents' income, education, and residential environment. We are hesitant to overinterpret these null findings and hope that future research will further examine these issues.

These null findings notwithstanding, our results do show that people of different ages conceptualize differently both dimensions (O'Grady, 2023). Mitteregger (2024) recently noted that "more recently socialized voters experienced their formative years in an era in which issues from the sociocultural dimension have become the main subject of political conflicts," expecting a difference in the salience of cultural issues across generations. Our analyses add nuance to this debate about cross-generational attitudinal differences, showing that age matters not only in setting the importance of cultural versus economic issues but also in how voters make sense of what these dimensions stand for.

The age divide is especially striking with regard to the cultural dimension, where immigration plays a strong role in older respondents' thinking about the cultural divide, while issues of gender and discrimination on the basis of sexual identities are prevalent among younger respondents. While there is no question that concerns over the demarcation of national boundaries have played a key role in shaping the cultural politics of Western polities over the last three decades (Kriesi et al., 2008; Norris and Inglehart, 2019), younger voters may be more invested in other types of cultural contestation. Our results suggest, albeit speculatively, that there is an inter-generational culture war over the question of what are the issues over which culture wars should be fought. Future work should consider where and why this age-based divide is deeper and explore its implications for the challenges of mainstream parties to maintain cross-generational coalitions in the context of the growing salience of cultural politics (Hall et al., 2023).

We also uncovered differences across the left–right divide and party support in the issues people associate with the economic and cultural dimensions. Voters across ideological and party lines differ not only in their positions on these dimensions, as scholars have previously shown, but also more fundamentally in how they make sense of them. We find that thinking about the cultural and economic dimensions in terms of immigration is predictive of support for radical right parties, while associating the cultural dimension with environmentalism is more common among supporters of green parties. As already discussed, our analyses do not claim to uncover the causal direction of this relationship. Our research objective here is limited to uncovering systematic differences in how people reason about politics across ideological and partisan fault lines.

Lastly, we have sought to demonstrate that while the economic and cultural dimensions are analytically distinct – they are intimately intertwined in people's understanding of politics. We have seen this already in the results of the cross-national analyses, where both immigration and green policies are mentioned in the context of both the economic and cultural dimensions – and welfare policies were raised in the context of the cultural dimension. Then, guided by ethnographic research (Cramer, 2012), we zoomed in on the issue of inequality and documented how it is inflected through both economic and cultural interpretations. This was especially pronounced among right-wing supporters, who believe that their governments discriminate against them in terms of the distribution of material resources while prioritizing culturally defined groups (mostly, though not exclusively, immigrants).

These findings are in line with recent calls to move beyond "the unhelpful economic versus cultural dichotomy" (Bolet, 2021, 2023). Previous work has already underscored the importance of considering how economic and cultural developments together interact in shaping political behavior in general and voting in particular (Gidron and Hall, 2017, 2020); nevertheless, these analyses did not dispute the basic distinction between the two dimensions of electoral politics. The findings we reported above go a step further by showing that the basic distinction between economic and cultural issues is relatively blurred in people's thinking about disagreements in the partisan arena.

A radical interpretation of our findings may suggest that if indeed the "new politics" issues of immigration and environmentalism continue to gain importance in shaping electoral competition, the two-dimensional framework may lose its potency as a theoretical construct in the analyses of comparative electoral behavior (at least within the context of developed democracies). If the key political issues of the day are understood by the public as both economic and cultural, then this distinction may become less attractive in the analysis of electoral competition. While we find this line of reasoning attractive, it may also be premature, given how generative the two-dimensional framework has proved for analysts of comparative electoral behavior. There is also no clear contender to replacing this framework for those who wish to position parties and voters within the same ideological space. More narrowly, we hope this Element advances our understanding of how this framework operates differently across contexts and would help scholars apply it with caution.

## 5.2 Limitations and Opportunities

There are several ways in which our theoretical framework and empirical design could and should be expanded. Our case selection covers countries from across Europe, next to the United States. We did not detect a clear pattern of American exceptionalism in terms of how the economic and cultural dimensions are seen from voters' perspectives – which should give encouragement to efforts of examining American electoral politics from a comparative perspective (Drutman, 2020; Kuo, 2019; Lieberman et al., 2019; Weyland, 2020; Weyland and Madrid, 2019).

Future work should expand the geographic scope of our analyses and consider whether our findings are generalizable beyond the universe of Western democracies. The two-dimensional framework has been used to analyze public opinion in all regions of the world, from Ghana through Yemen to Japan (Malka et al., 2019). We have limited ourselves to the advanced democracies for theoretical and practical reasons, yet the basic motivation behind our work – better understanding how citizens make sense of key political dimensions – is also relevant to other contexts.

Our analyses are limited not only geographically but also temporally, providing us with only a snapshot in time. It may be the case that events such as economic crises, wars, and environmental disasters change the ways people think about the economic and cultural dimensions. For instance, Jankowski et al. (2023) show that the meanings German political elites (candidates running for office) attribute to the left–right divide in open-ended responses change over time in response to political developments. And considering that political elites tend to have a more stable understanding of politics (Kinder and Kalmoe, 2017), it is only reasonable to assume that such shifts in the understanding of politics are even more common and more pronounced among the general public. And it is worth mentioning that our data was collected during the outbreak of the COVID-19, which had multiple social, economic, and also political repercussions (Gadarian et al., 2022). Investigating such temporal fluctuations in people's understanding of the ideological space remains for future research.

Methodologically, we acknowledge that there is not yet agreed-upon best practices for the analyses of open-ended survey questions collected across multiple countries and languages.[11] This is why we strove to be as transparent as possible and to elaborate on the various decisions we made throughout the empirical analyses (Table 7). This should make it easier for others to reanalyze our data: for instance, it is possible to aggregate the multiple topics into different categories and construct different dictionaries. And scholars analyzing other datasets may find the methodological road map helpful and could hopefully improve it.

---

[11] For a comprehensive and useful step in this direction in economics, although with less of an emphasis on cross-national variations, see Haaland et al. (2024).

Lastly, our analyses demonstrate the infinite opportunities that lie in the analyses of open-ended questions, for descriptive work and potentially also for causal inference – opportunities that are likely to multiply with the application of Artificial Intelligence to automated text analysis. Large-scale comparative surveys, such as the Comparative Study of Electoral Systems, have not yet fully taken on this opportunity of inviting respondents to open a window to their understanding of politics using their own words. We hope our analyses, which follow and build upon recent advances in the field (Condon and Wichowsky, 2020; Ferrario and Stantcheva, 2022; Stantcheva, 2022, 2024; Zollinger, 2024), will encourage more research of this type. Better understanding how ordinary citizens make sense of politics is a foundational challenge for social scientists, and we are now better positioned to address it – as we hope this Element demonstrates.

# Appendix A
## Descriptives

Figure A.1 presents the percentage of stand-alone mentions of a topic. The figure shows that the prompts likely had some effect on how respondents answered the open-ended questions. Specifically, it visualizes the proportion of responses discussing multiple topics for each of the identified topics in the cultural and economic dimensions. Participants were more likely to discuss the two categories mentioned in the prompts – immigration and inequality – in isolation, without including other topics. In the cultural dimension, about 41% of the responses that mention immigration also discuss other topics, while about 61% of the responses that mention the environment include other issues. The difference is less pronounced in the economic dimension: On average, 51% of responses that mention inequality include other topics, while the figure is 66% for responses about the labor market.

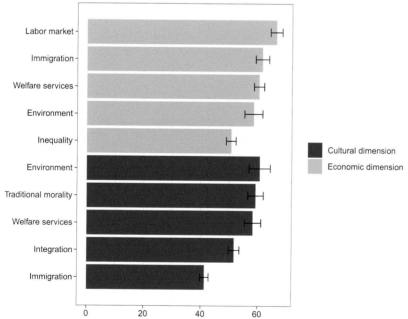

**Figure A.1** Percentage of stand-alone mentions of a topic
**Note:** For each topic, this figure visualizes the share of responses discussing multiple topics. Whiskers indicate 95% confidence interval around the mean.

# Appendix B
## *BERTopic Results*

To detect topics in the open-ended responses, we employ BERTopic (Grootendorst, 2022). Figures B.1 and B.2 present the frequency of detected topics in the cultural and economic condition, respectively. Classified topics are colored, topics that could not be classified in one of the five topics per condition are displayed in grey. Topics that related to "don't know" answers were removed.

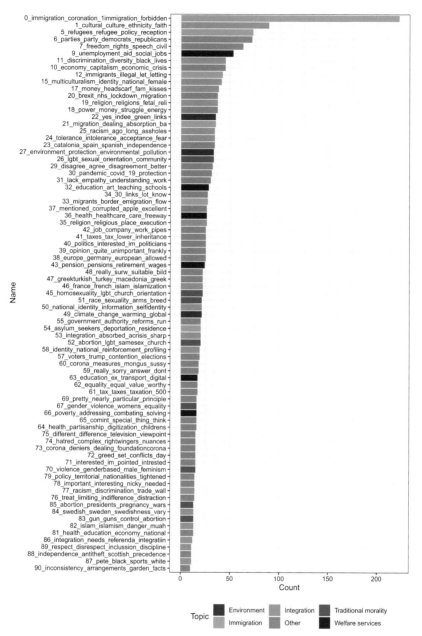

**Figure B.1** Topic modeling results (cultural dimension)

**Note**: Shows topic labels provided by BERTopic. Unlabeled responses and topics that relate to *Dont Know* answers were removed from the plot.

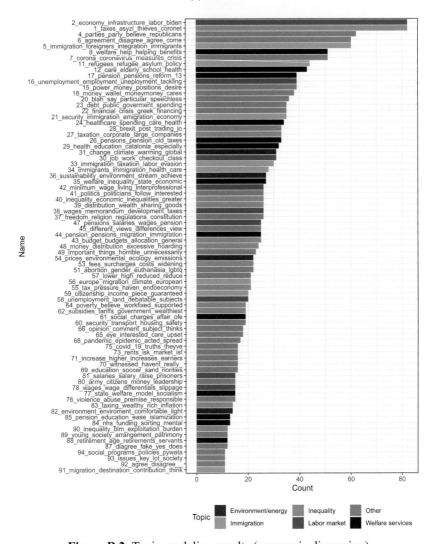

**Figure B.2** Topic modeling results (economic dimension)

**Note**: Shows topic labels provided by BERTopic. Unlabeled responses and topics that relate to *Dont Know* answers were removed from the plot.

# Appendix C
## *Dictionaries*

Tables C.1 and C.2 display the keywords used to classify responses into topics in each condition.

**Table C.1** Dictionary for cultural dimension categories

| Category | Word list |
|---|---|
| **Immigration** | 1immigration, Africans, aliens, asylum, birthright, border, borders, citizen, citizens, citizenship, deportation, deported, emigrants, emigrate, emigration, foreign, foreigner, foreigners, fugitive, iimmigration, ilegal, illegal, imigrants, imigration, immigration, immigrant, immigrants, immigration, immigrations, immigrationsecuritythe, immigrationsexual, immigraxion, illegals, imgration, inmigation, iussoli, jiusoli, migrant, migrants, migrantsrefugees, migration, migratory, moroccan, moroccans, morocco, natives, newcomers, passport, passports, prerefugeeimmigration, refugee, refugees, securityeconomyborder, seeker, seekers, soli, visas |
| **Integration** | alah, alm, antisemitic, antisemitism, appropriation, assimilate, assimilation, black, blacklives, blacks, blm, bullfighting, bulls, burqa, clan, clans, cohesion, color, colour, cultura, cultural, culturality, culturally, culture, cultureculturality, cultures, custom, customs, discrimination, diversity, ethnic, ethnicity, ethnika, eurasian, festivals, ghettoisation, headscarf, hellenism, heritage, homeland, identity, identity, inclusion, inclusive, inclusiveness, inclussion, integrate, integrated, integratiin, integration, intergration, internationalism, intolerance, intregation, islam, islamic, islamism, islamist, islamists, islamization, islamphobia, jehovah, jewish, jewishness, jews, minorities, minority, mosque, multicultural, multiculturalism, multiculturiamism, multiculturism, multiracialism, muslim, nation, national, nationalism, nationalist, nationalities, nationality, nations, nontolerance, nonwhiteenglish, otherness, patriotism, patriots, pete, piet, plurinationality, prejudice, prejudices |
| **Integration cont'd** | race, raceism, races, racial, racism, racist, racists, rascism, rascism, segregation, skin, stigmatization, subculture, subcultures, supremacy, swedishness, tolerance, toleranceintolerance, tolerances, tradition, traditions, white, whites, xenophobia, xenos |

| Category | Terms |
|---|---|
| **Tradition/Morality** | abortion, abortions, atheists, catholic, christian, christianity, church, clergy, dogma, elgiebt, ethics, euthanasia, exual, faith, faiths, female, feminism, feminist, fetal, gay, gays, gayslesbians, gender, genderbased, genders, homobitransphobia, homophobia, homosexuality, homosexuals, immigrationsexual, invitro, lbgt, lesbians, lgbt, lgbtq, lgbtqi, lgbtqia, lgtb, marriage, marriages, morals, orientation, patriarchies, polygamy, pregnancy, religion, religionextremism, religions, religious, reproduction, samesex, sectarianism, secular, secularism, sex, sexism, sexist, sexual, sexuality, singleparent, statusreligion, vitro, woman, women, womens, worship |
| **Welfare services** | aid, allowance, allowances, assistance, benefit, benefits, childcare, delivery, dental, education, elderly, entitled, entitlement, hartz, harz, health, healthcare, homelessness, hospitals, housing, insurance, kindergartens, museums, nhs, pension, pensionageing, pensioners, pensions, recipients, relief, remuneration, retirement, retirements, school, schooling, schools, service, services, spending, stimulus, subsidies, subsidy, support, supports, surcharge, surcharges, welfare, welfarism |
| **Environment** | agriculture, animal, animals, climate, climates, eco, ecological, ecology, ecosystem, electromobility, energies, energy, environment, environmental, environmentally, farmer, farming, flights, fuel, gas, green, methana, methane, nature, nitrogen, nuclear, pipeline, planet, pollution, railways, renewable, trains, transition, transport, warming, warmingnew |

**Table C.2** Dictionary for economic dimension categories

| Category | Word list |
|---|---|
| **Inequality** | burden, burdens, capitalism, capitalist, class, classes, corporate, corporation, corporations, disparities, disparity, distributed, distribution, divergence, enrich, enriching, equal, equality, equally, equalrights, equity, eviction, evictions, highincome, homelessness, impoverish, impuestos, inequalities, inequality, inequalitycitizenship, inheritance, lowincome, megacorporation, mental, poor, poorer, poorest, poorthe, poverty, precariousness, redistribution, rich, richer, richest, tax, taxation, taxes, taxesloans, taxesmess, taxfree, taxing, taxpayer, taxpayers, twoearners, underprivileged, unequal, unfair, unfairly, wealth, wealthier, wealthiest, wealthy |
| **Welfare services** | 500, 500plus, aid, aids, alg2, allowance, allowances, assistance, asylum, asyzl, benefitdependent, benefits, benefitsimmigration, benifits, charges, compensation, coverage, daycare, doctors, education, elderly, entitlement, entitlements, handicapped, hardships, hartz, hartziv, health, healthcare, hospital, housing, hunger, illness, immigrationworkhealth, insurance, medical, medicalthe, medicare, nhs, penions, pension, pensioners, pensionew, pensions, recipients, retirees, retirement, retirements, school, schoolcarehospital, schooling, schoolkids, senior, service, services, servicesbusinesses, shelter, spending, spendings, subsidies, subsidy, supplements, surcharge, surcharges, wagesbenefitssurcharges, welfare, welfarism, welfarist, wellfare, workbenefit |
| **Labor market** | 8hour, employee, employees, employers, employment, hours, immigrationworkhealth, income, incomebased, incomes, insecurity, job, jobs, jobwise, labor, labour, payroll, salaries, salario, salary, selfemployed, unemployed, unemployment, uneployment, union, unionism, unions, unpaid, wage, wagecarpet, wages, wagesbenefitssurcharges, work, workbenefit, worker, workers, working, works, workshop, workwages |

| | |
|---|---|
| **Immigration** | aliens, benefitsimmigration, black, blm, border, borders, citizenship, citizenstate, cultural, culturality, culture, emigrants, emigration, foreign, foreigners, illegal, illegals, imigrants, imigrate, imigration, immigrant, immigrants, immigration, immigrationworkhealth, immigrtants, inequalitycitizenship, integration, intergeation, intergration, intigration, islam, islamization, migrants, migration, minorities, muslims, race, races, racial, racism, racist, rasism, refugee, refugees, religion, religious, segregation, soli, templesplace, worship |
| **Environment/Energy** | agriculture, bentzin, climat, climate, diesel, drilling, eco, ecologia, ecological, ecology, emissions, enviroment, environment, environmental, environmentally, environmentandeconomy, farmers, food, fuel, garbage, gas, gases, gasoline, green, greenhouse, nitrogen, nuclear, petroldiesel, petroleum, phaseout, plants, pollution, renewable, sustainability, sustainable, traffic, transport, transportation, vehicle, warming |

# Appendix D

## *Further Analyses*

Tables D.1 and D.2 provide further robustness checks. Similar to Tables 12 and 13, we check the predictive power of the discussed topics. In contrast to the two tables in the main body of the text, we regress self-reported vote choice in Tables D.1 and D.2 on topic dummies and covariates.

**Table D.1** Predicting vote choice with mentioned topics (cultural dimension)

| | Left–right scale | Ecological | Left | Social-Dem. | Liberal | Christian-Dem. | Conservative | Nationalist |
|---|---|---|---|---|---|---|---|---|
| (Intercept) | 4.796*** | 0.114*** | 0.111*** | 0.183*** | 0.108*** | 0.253*** | 0.006 | 0.014 |
| | (0.211) | (0.013) | (0.019) | (0.029) | (0.021) | (0.018) | (0.025) | (0.024) |
| Immigration | 0.072 | 0.003 | 0.009 | −0.010 | −0.003 | −0.003 | 0.020 | 0.068*** |
| | (0.121) | (0.007) | (0.011) | (0.016) | (0.012) | (0.010) | (0.014) | (0.014) |
| Tradition/morality | −0.532** | −0.003 | 0.013 | 0.032 | 0.037* | 0.008 | −0.031 | −0.003 |
| | (0.185) | (0.011) | (0.016) | (0.025) | (0.019) | (0.016) | (0.022) | (0.021) |
| Environment | −0.037 | 0.043** | −0.024 | 0.032 | 0.061** | 0.005 | −0.014 | −0.028 |
| | (0.232) | (0.014) | (0.021) | (0.031) | (0.024) | (0.020) | (0.028) | (0.026) |
| Integration | −0.345* | 0.015+ | 0.008 | 0.012 | 0.012 | 0.009 | −0.014 | 0.021 |
| | (0.142) | (0.009) | (0.013) | (0.019) | (0.014) | (0.012) | (0.017) | (0.016) |
| Welfare services | −0.055 | −0.009 | 0.043** | 0.023 | 0.025 | 0.038* | −0.019 | 0.022 |
| | (0.186) | (0.011) | (0.016) | (0.025) | (0.019) | (0.016) | (0.022) | (0.021) |
| Age | 0.036 | −0.003 | 0.003 | 0.007 | 0.011* | 0.007+ | 0.036*** | 0.017** |
| | (0.046) | (0.003) | (0.004) | (0.006) | (0.005) | (0.004) | (0.005) | (0.005) |
| Age squared | −0.057 | 0.003 | −0.002 | −0.019** | 0.000 | −0.003 | 0.006 | −0.006 |
| | (0.045) | (0.003) | (0.004) | (0.006) | (0.005) | (0.004) | (0.005) | (0.005) |
| Male | 0.314*** | −0.015** | 0.009 | 0.009 | 0.000 | −0.001 | 0.017 | 0.030** |
| | (0.089) | (0.005) | (0.008) | (0.012) | (0.009) | (0.008) | (0.011) | (0.010) |
| Medium education | 0.102 | −0.022* | −0.019 | −0.039* | −0.051*** | −0.020 | 0.002 | 0.013 |
| | (0.144) | (0.009) | (0.013) | (0.020) | (0.015) | (0.012) | (0.017) | (0.016) |
| Low education | −0.095 | −0.007 | −0.022* | −0.025+ | −0.046*** | −0.010 | −0.007 | 0.051*** |
| | (0.102) | (0.006) | (0.009) | (0.014) | (0.010) | (0.009) | (0.012) | (0.011) |

**Table D.1** (Cont.)

| | | | | | | | |
|---|---|---|---|---|---|---|---|
| No education | 0.168 | −0.032* | −0.025 | −0.010 | −0.080** | −0.033 | −0.063* | −0.008 |
| | (0.250) | (0.015) | (0.022) | (0.034) | (0.025) | (0.021) | (0.030) | (0.028) |
| Rural | 0.061 | 0.001 | 0.013 | −0.049*** | −0.016 | −0.008 | 0.012 | 0.024* |
| | (0.101) | (0.006) | (0.009) | (0.014) | (0.010) | (0.009) | (0.012) | (0.011) |
| Medium HH inc | −0.398** | 0.003 | 0.015 | −0.015 | −0.033* | −0.025* | −0.032+ | −0.005 |
| | (0.138) | (0.008) | (0.012) | (0.019) | (0.014) | (0.012) | (0.016) | (0.015) |
| Low HH inc | −0.348* | 0.007 | 0.011 | −0.020 | −0.028+ | −0.003 | −0.012 | 0.014 |
| | (0.155) | (0.009) | (0.014) | (0.021) | (0.016) | (0.013) | (0.019) | (0.017) |
| HH inc missing | −0.613** | −0.012 | 0.003 | −0.060* | −0.048* | −0.050** | −0.040+ | −0.050* |
| | (0.191) | (0.011) | (0.017) | (0.026) | (0.019) | (0.016) | (0.023) | (0.021) |
| Two topics | −0.224 | −0.002 | −0.003 | −0.006 | −0.018 | −0.031+ | −0.002 | −0.064** |
| | (0.202) | (0.012) | (0.018) | (0.027) | (0.021) | (0.017) | (0.024) | (0.023) |
| Three or more topics | 0.015 | −0.003 | 0.025 | −0.020 | −0.113** | −0.014 | 0.111* | −0.065 |
| | (0.393) | (0.024) | (0.035) | (0.053) | (0.040) | (0.033) | (0.047) | (0.044) |
| Num.Obs. | 3,471 | 3,471 | 3,471 | 3,471 | 3,471 | 3,471 | 3,471 | 3,471 |
| R2 | 0.045 | 0.053 | 0.054 | 0.112 | 0.137 | 0.175 | 0.117 | 0.078 |
| R2 Adj. | 0.038 | 0.046 | 0.047 | 0.105 | 0.131 | 0.169 | 0.110 | 0.071 |
| Country–FE included | yes | yes | yes | yes | yes | yes | yes | yes |

**Note:** $+p < 0.1$, $*p < 0.05$, $**p < 0.01$, $***p < 0.001$. Coefficients estimated based on OLS regression in column 1 and linear probability models in columns 2–8. For topics, education and income levels, and number of topics mentioned, the reference categories are "none of the defined topic mentioned," "High education," "High income," and "1 or none of the topics mentioned." Age variables are standardized.

**Table D.2** Predicting vote choice with mentioned topics (economic dimension)

| | Left–right scale | Ecological | Left | Social-Dem. | Liberal | Christian-Dem. | Conservative | Nationalist |
|---|---|---|---|---|---|---|---|---|
| (Intercept) | 4.880*** | 0.166*** | 0.062*** | 0.150*** | 0.063** | 0.204*** | 0.010 | 0.046* |
| | (0.209) | (0.014) | (0.017) | (0.028) | (0.021) | (0.017) | (0.025) | (0.023) |
| Welfare services | −0.282* | 0.004 | 0.018 | 0.026 | −0.003 | 0.004 | 0.028 | −0.013 |
| | (0.142) | (0.010) | (0.012) | (0.019) | (0.014) | (0.012) | (0.017) | (0.015) |
| Immigration | 0.420* | −0.013 | −0.015 | −0.008 | −0.005 | 0.015 | 0.020 | 0.117*** |
| | (0.165) | (0.011) | (0.013) | (0.022) | (0.017) | (0.014) | (0.020) | (0.018) |
| Inequality | −0.431*** | 0.000 | 0.011 | 0.066*** | 0.012 | 0.002 | −0.003 | 0.001 |
| | (0.129) | (0.009) | (0.010) | (0.017) | (0.013) | (0.011) | (0.016) | (0.014) |
| Labor market | 0.140 | 0.001 | −0.005 | 0.019 | −0.018 | 0.015 | 0.055** | −0.021 |
| | (0.163) | (0.011) | (0.013) | (0.022) | (0.017) | (0.014) | (0.020) | (0.018) |
| Environment/energy | −0.424* | 0.022 | −0.002 | 0.033 | 0.012 | −0.011 | −0.001 | −0.021 |
| | (0.203) | (0.014) | (0.017) | (0.027) | (0.021) | (0.017) | (0.025) | (0.022) |
| Age | 0.089* | 0.002 | 0.003 | 0.013* | 0.002 | 0.003 | 0.032*** | 0.015** |
| | (0.044) | (0.003) | (0.004) | (0.006) | (0.005) | (0.004) | (0.005) | (0.005) |
| Age squared | −0.219*** | 0.001 | −0.005 | −0.005 | 0.002 | 0.000 | 0.010+ | −0.016** |
| | (0.045) | (0.003) | (0.004) | (0.006) | (0.005) | (0.004) | (0.005) | (0.005) |
| Male | 0.363*** | 0.001 | 0.012+ | 0.008 | 0.006 | −0.007 | −0.008 | 0.053*** |
| | (0.087) | (0.006) | (0.007) | (0.012) | (0.009) | (0.007) | (0.011) | (0.010) |
| Medium education | −0.055 | −0.019+ | −0.001 | −0.056** | −0.048*** | −0.024* | −0.009 | 0.027+ |
| | (0.141) | (0.010) | (0.012) | (0.019) | (0.014) | (0.012) | (0.017) | (0.015) |
| Low education | 0.060 | −0.024*** | 0.003 | −0.048*** | −0.031** | −0.005 | −0.002 | 0.043*** |
| | (0.099) | (0.007) | (0.008) | (0.013) | (0.010) | (0.008) | (0.012) | (0.011) |

**Table D.2** (Cont.)

| | | | | | | | |
|---|---|---|---|---|---|---|---|
| No education | 0.492+ | −0.035+ | 0.010 | −0.049 | −0.110*** | −0.013 | −0.013 | 0.023 |
| | (0.257) | (0.018) | (0.021) | (0.035) | (0.026) | (0.022) | (0.031) | (0.028) |
| Rural | 0.305** | −0.009 | −0.009 | −0.040** | 0.000 | 0.009 | 0.051*** | 0.011 |
| | (0.101) | (0.007) | (0.008) | (0.013) | (0.010) | (0.008) | (0.012) | (0.011) |
| Medium HH inc | −0.371** | −0.007 | 0.002 | 0.008 | −0.018 | −0.016 | −0.038* | −0.003 |
| | (0.137) | (0.009) | (0.011) | (0.018) | (0.014) | (0.011) | (0.017) | (0.015) |
| Low HH inc | −0.336* | 0.003 | −0.007 | 0.000 | 0.014 | 0.002 | −0.038* | 0.015 |
| | (0.150) | (0.010) | (0.012) | (0.020) | (0.015) | (0.013) | (0.018) | (0.016) |
| HH inc missing | −0.319+ | −0.022+ | −0.009 | −0.054* | −0.020 | −0.020 | −0.053* | −0.002 |
| | (0.187) | (0.013) | (0.015) | (0.025) | (0.019) | (0.016) | (0.023) | (0.020) |
| Two topics | −0.023 | 0.005 | 0.010 | −0.023 | 0.021 | −0.005 | −0.014 | −0.013 |
| | (0.199) | (0.014) | (0.016) | (0.027) | (0.020) | (0.017) | (0.024) | (0.022) |
| Three or more topics | 0.223 | 0.020 | 0.037 | −0.102* | 0.015 | −0.021 | −0.049 | 0.045 |
| | (0.345) | (0.024) | (0.028) | (0.046) | (0.035) | (0.029) | (0.042) | (0.038) |
| Num.Obs. | 3,594 | 3,594 | 3,594 | 3,594 | 3,594 | 3,594 | 3,594 | 3,594 |
| R2 | 0.041 | 0.071 | 0.047 | 0.121 | 0.134 | 0.183 | 0.112 | 0.076 |
| R2 Adj. | 0.034 | 0.064 | 0.040 | 0.115 | 0.128 | 0.177 | 0.105 | 0.069 |
| Country-FE included | yes | yes | yes | yes | yes | yes | yes | yes |

**Note:** $+p < 0.1$, $*p < 0.05$, $**p < 0.01$, $***p < 0.001$. Coefficients estimated based on OLS regression in column 1 and linear probability models in columns 2–8. For topics, education and income levels, and number of topics mentioned, the reference categories are "none of the defined topic mentioned," "High education," "High income," and "1 or none of the topics mentioned." Age variables are standardized.

# References

Abou-Chadi, T., Cohen, D., and Wagner, M. (2022). The centre-right versus the radical right: The role of migration issues and economic grievances. *Journal of Ethnic and Migration Studies*, 48(2):366–384.

Abou-Chadi, T. and Wagner, M. (2020). Electoral fortunes of social democratic parties: Do second dimension positions matter? *Journal of European Public Policy*, 27(2):246–272.

Adorno, T., Frenkel-Brunswick, E., Levinson, D., and Sanford, N. (1950). *The authoritarian personality*. Harper.

Aspide, A., Brown, K. J., DiGiuseppe, M., and Slaski, A. (2023). Age and support for public debt reduction. *European Journal of Political Research*, 62(4): 1191–1211.

Bakker, R., De Vries, C., Edwards, E., et al. (2015). Measuring party positions in Europe: The chapel hill expert survey trend file, 1999–2010. *Party Politics*, 21(1):143–152.

Bakker, R., Jolly, S., and Polk, J. (2022). Analyzing the cross-national comparability of party positions on the socio-cultural and EU dimensions in Europe. *Political Science Research and Methods*, 10(2):408–418.

Bakker, R., Jolly, S., Polk, J., and Poole, K. (2014). The European common space: Extending the use of anchoring vignettes. *The Journal of Politics*, 76(4):1089–1101.

Baldassarri, D. and Goldberg, A. (2014). Neither ideologues nor agnostics: Alternative voters' belief system in an age of partisan politics. *American Journal of Sociology*, 120(1):45–95.

Bale, T. and Kaltwasser, C. R. (2021). *Riding the populist wave: Europe's mainstream right in crisis*. Cambridge University Press.

Barberá, P., Casas, A., Nagler, J., et al. (2019). Who leads? Who follows? Measuring issue attention and agenda setting by legislators and the mass public using social media data. *American Political Science Review*, 113(4):883–901.

Bartolini, S. (2000). *The political mobilization of the European left, 1860–1980: The class cleavage*. Cambridge University Press.

Benoit, K. and Laver, M. (2006). *Party policy in modern democracies*. Routledge.

Beramendi, P., Häusermann, S., Kitschelt, H., and Kriesi, H. (2015). *The politics of advanced capitalism*. Cambridge University Press.

Bobbio, N. (1996). *Left and right: The significance of a political distinction.* University of Chicago Press.

Bochsler, D., Green, E., Jenne, E., Mylonas, H., and Wimmer, A. (2021). Exchange on the quantitative measurement of ethnic and national identity. *Nations and Nationalism*, 27(1):22–40.

Bolet, D. (2021). Drinking alone: Local socio-cultural degradation and radical right support – the case of British pub closures. *Comparative Political Studies*, 54(9):1653–1692.

Bolet, D. (2023). The janus-faced nature of radical voting: Subjective social decline at the roots of radical right and radical left support. *Party Politics*, 29(3):475–488.

Bonikowski, B., Luo, Y., and Stuhler, O. (2022). Politics as usual? Measuring populism, nationalism, and authoritarianism in US presidential campaigns (1952–2020) with neural language models. *Sociological Methods & Research*, 51(4):1721–1787.

Bormann, N.-C. and Golder, M. (2013). Democratic electoral systems around the world, 1946–2011. *Electoral Studies*, 32(2):360–369.

Bornschier, S. (2010a). *Cleavage politics and the populist right: The new cultural conflict in Western Europe.* Temple University Press.

Bornschier, S. (2010b). The new cultural divide and the two-dimensional political space in Western Europe. *West European Politics*, 33(3):419–444.

Bremer, B. and Rennwald, L. (2023). Who still likes social democracy? The support base of social democratic parties reconsidered. *Party Politics*, 29(4): 741–754.

Carmines, E. G. and D'Amico, N. J. (2015). The new look in political ideology research. *Annual Review of Political Science*, 18:205–216.

Caughey, D., O'Grady, T., and Warshaw, C. (2019). Policy ideology in European mass publics, 1981–2016. *American Political Science Review*, 113(3): 674–693.

Cavaillé, C. and Trump, K.-S. (2015). The two facets of social policy preferences. *The Journal of Politics*, 77(1):146–160.

Colantone, I., Di Lonardo, L., Margalit, Y., and Percoco, M. (2024). The political consequences of green policies: Evidence from Italy. *American Political Science Review*, 118(1): 108–126.

Condon, M. and Wichowsky, A. (2020). *The economic other: Inequality in the American political imagination.* University of Chicago Press.

Cramer, K. J. (2012). Putting inequality in its place: Rural consciousness and the power of perspective. *American Political Science Review*, 106(3): 517–532.

Cramer, K. J. (2016). *The politics of resentment: Rural consciousness in Wisconsin and the rise of Scott Walker.* University of Chicago Press.

Dalton, R. J. (2010). Left–right orientations, context, and voting choices. In *Citizens, context, and choice: How context shapes citizens' electoral choices,* eds. Russell J. Dalton and Christopher J. Anderson. Oxford University Press. pages 103–125.

Dancygier, R. M. and Margalit, Y. (2020). The evolution of the immigration debate: Evidence from a new dataset of party positions over the last half-century. *Comparative Political Studies,* 53(5):734–774.

Dancygier, R. M. and Donnelly, M. J. (2013). Sectoral economies, economic contexts, and attitudes toward immigration. *The Journal of Politics,* 75(1):17–35.

Dassonneville, R. (2021). Change and continuity in the ideological gender gap a longitudinal analysis of left-right self-placement in OECD countries. *European Journal of Political Research,* 60(1):225–238.

Dassonneville, R., Fournier, P., and Somer-Topcu, Z. (2023). Partisan attachments in a multidimensional space. *West European Politics,* 46(4): 678–704.

De Vries, C. E., Hobolt, S. B., Proksch, S.-O., and Slapin, J. B. (2021). *Foundations of European politics: A comparative approach.* Oxford University Press.

Devlin, J., Chang, M.-W., Lee, K., and Toutanova, K. (2018). Bert: Pre-training of deep bidirectional transformers for language understanding. *arXiv preprint arXiv:1810.04805.*

Diamond, E. P. (2023). Understanding rural identities and environmental policy attitudes in America. *Perspectives on Politics,* 21(2): 502–518.

Diamond, P. and Chwalisz, C. (2015). *The predistribution agenda: Tackling inequality and supporting sustainable growth.* Bloomsbury.

Dolezal, M., Eder, N., Kritzinger, S., and Zeglovits, E. (2013). The structure of issue attitudes revisited: A dimensional analysis of Austrian voters and party elites. *Journal of Elections, Public Opinion & Parties,* 23(4):423–443.

Drutman, L. (2020). *Breaking the two-party doom loop: The case for multiparty democracy in America.* Oxford University Press.

Ferrario, B. and Stantcheva, S. (2022). Eliciting people's first-order concerns: Text analysis of open-ended survey questions. *AEA Papers and Proceedings,* 112:163–169.

Ford, R. and Jennings, W. (2020). The changing cleavage politics of Western Europe. *Annual Review of Political Science,* 23:295–314.

Gadarian, S. K., Goodman, S. W., and Pepinsky, T. B. (2022). *Pandemic politics: The deadly toll of partisanship in the age of COVID.* Princeton University Press.

Gerring, J. (2012). Mere description. *British Journal of Political Science,* 42(4):721–746.

Gest, J. (2016). *The new minority: White working class politics in an age of immigration and inequality*. Oxford University Press.

Gethin, A., Martínez-Toledano, C., and Piketty, T. (2022). Brahmin left versus merchant right: Changing political cleavages in 21 western democracies, 1948–2020. *The Quarterly Journal of Economics*, 137(1):1–48.

Gidron, N. (2022). Many ways to be right: Cross-pressured voters in Western Europe. *British Journal of Political Science*, 52(1):146–161.

Gidron, N. and Hall, P. A. (2017). The politics of social status: Economic and cultural roots of the populist right. *The British Journal of Sociology*, 68: S57–S84.

Gidron, N. and Hall, P. A. (2020). Populism as a problem of social integration. *Comparative Political Studies*, 53(7):1027–1059.

Gidron, N., Sheffer, L., and Mor, G. (2022). Validating the feeling thermometer as a measure of partisan affect in multi-party systems. *Electoral Studies*, 80: 102542.

Gidron, N. and Ziblatt, D. (2019). Center-right political parties in advanced democracies. *Annual Review of Political Science*, 22:17–35.

Givens, T. and Luedtke, A. (2005). European immigration policies in comparative perspective: Issue salience, partisanship and immigrant rights. *Comparative European Politics*, 3(1):1–22.

Gonthier, F. and Guerra, T. (2023). How party polarization shapes the structuring of policy preferences in Europe. *Party Politics*, 29(2): 384–393.

Grootendorst, M. (2022). Bertopic: Neural topic modeling with a class-based tf-idf procedure. *arXiv preprint arXiv:2203.05794*.

Haaland, I. K., Roth, C., Stantcheva, S., and Wohlfart, J. (2024). Measuring what is top of mind. *National Bureau of Economic Research*, w32421.

Hainmueller, J. and Hopkins, D. J. (2014). Public attitudes toward immigration. *Annual Review of Political Science*, 17: 225–249.

Hall, P. A. (2013). The political origins of our economic discontents. In *Politics in the new hard times: The great recession in comparative perspective*, eds. Miles Kahler and David A. Lake. pages 129–149. Cornell University Press.

Hall, P. A. (2020). The electoral politics of growth regimes. *Perspectives on Politics*, 18(1):185–199.

Hall, P. A., Evans, G., and Kim, S. I. (2023). *Political change and electoral coalitions in western democracies*. Cambridge University Press.

Häusermann, S. and Kriesi, H. (2015). What do voters want? Dimensions and configurations in individual-level preferences and party choice. In *The politics of advanced capitalism*, eds. Hanspeter Kriesi, Herbert Kitschelt, Pablo Beramendi, and Silja Häusermann. pages 202–230. Cambridge University Press.

Häusermann, S., Pinggera, M., Ares, M., and Enggist, M. (2022). Class and social policy in the knowledge economy. *European Journal of Political Research*, 61(2):462–484.

Hillen, S. and Steiner, N. D. (2020). The consequences of supply gaps in two-dimensional policy spaces for voter turnout and political support: The case of economically left-wing and culturally right-wing citizens in Western Europe. *European Journal of Political Research*, 59(2):331–353.

Hooghe, L. and Marks, G. (2018). Cleavage theory meets Europe's crises: Lipset, Rokkan, and the transnational cleavage. *Journal of European Public Policy*, 25(1):109–135.

Hooghe, L., Marks, G., and Wilson, C. J. (2002). Does left/right structure party positions on European integration? *Comparative Political Studies*, 35(8):965–989.

Hutter, S. and Kriesi, H. (2019). *European party politics in times of crisis*. Cambridge University Press.

Inglehart, R. (1984). The changing structure of political cleavages in western society. In *Electoral change in advanced industrial democracies: Realignment or dealignment?*, eds. Russell J. Dalton and Scott E. Flanagan, pages 25–69. Princeton University Press.

Inglehart, R. and Flanagan, S. C. (1987). Value change in industrial societies. *American Political Science Review*, 81(4):1289–1319.

Iversen, T. and Soskice, D. (2006). Electoral institutions and the politics of coalitions: Why some democracies redistribute more than others. *American Political Science Review*, 100(2):165–181.

Jankowski, M., Schneider, S. H., and Tepe, M. (2023). How stable are "left" and "right"? A morphological analysis using open-ended survey responses of parliamentary candidates. *Party Politics* 29(1): 26–39.

Jolly, S., Bakker, R., Hooghe, L., et al. (2022). Chapel hill expert survey trend file, 1999–2019. *Electoral Studies*, 75:102420.

Jost, J. T., Federico, C. M., and Napier, J. L. (2009). Political ideology: Its structure, functions, and elective affinities. *Annual Review of Psychology*, 60(1):307–337.

Kersch, K. I. (2011). Ecumenicalism through constitutionalism: The discursive development of constitutional conservatism in national review, 1955–1980. *Studies in American Political Development*, 25(1):86–116.

Kinder, D. R. and Kalmoe, N. P. (2017). *Neither liberal nor conservative: Ideological innocence in the American public*. University of Chicago Press.

Kitschelt, H. (1994). *The transformation of European social democracy*. Cambridge University Press.

Kitschelt, H. and Hellemans, S. (1990). The left-right semantics and the new politics cleavage. *Comparative Political Studies*, 23(2):210–238.

Kitschelt, H. and Rehm, P. (2014). Occupations as a site of political preference formation. *Comparative Political Studies*, 47(12):1670–1706.

Klüver, H. and Spoon, J.-J. (2016). Who responds? Voters, parties and issue attention. *British Journal of Political Science*, 46(3):633–654.

Koedam, J. (2022). A change of heart? Analysing stability and change in European party positions. *West European Politics*, 45(4):693–715.

Kriesi, H., Grande, E., Lachat, R., et .al. (2006). Globalization and the transformation of the national political space: Six European countries compared. *European Journal of Political Research*, 45(6):921–956.

Kriesi, H., Grande, E., Lachat, R., et al. (2008). *West European politics in the age of globalization*. Cambridge University Press.

Kuo, D. (2019). Comparing America: Reflections on democracy across subfields. *Perspectives on Politics*, 17(3):788–800.

Lamont, M. (2009). *The dignity of working men: Morality and the boundaries of race, class, and immigration*. Harvard University Press.

Lamont, M., Park, B. Y., and Ayala-Hurtado, E. (2017). Trump's electoral speeches and his appeal to the American white working class. *The British Journal of Sociology*, 68:S153–S180.

Lauterbach, F. and De Vries, C. E. (2020). Europe belongs to the young? Generational differences in public opinion towards the European Union during the Eurozone crisis. *Journal of European Public Policy*, 27(2):168–187.

Lefkofridi, Z., Wagner, M., and Willmann, J. E. (2014). Left-authoritarians and policy representation in Western Europe: Electoral choice across ideological dimensions. *West European Politics*, 37(1):65–90.

Lieberman, R. C., Mettler, S., Pepinsky, T. B., Roberts, K. M., and Valelly, R. (2019). The Trump presidency and American democracy: A historical and comparative analysis. *Perspectives on Politics*, 17(2):470–479.

Lipset, S. M. and Rokkan, S. (1990). Cleavage structures, party systems, and voter alignments: In *The west European party system*, Oxford readings in politics and government, ed. Peter Mair. Oxford [England]; New York: Oxford University Press, 91–138.

Lucas, C., Nielsen, R. A., Roberts, M. E., et al. (2015). Computer-assisted text analysis for comparative politics. *Political Analysis*, 23(2):254–277.

Malhotra, N., Margalit, Y., and Mo, C. H. (2013). Economic explanations for opposition to immigration: Distinguishing between prevalence and conditional impact. *American Journal of Political Science*, 57(2):391–410.

Malka, A., Lelkes, Y., and Soto, C. J. (2019). Are cultural and economic conservatism positively correlated? A large-scale cross-national test. *British Journal of Political Science*, 49(3):1045–1069.

Manow, P. (2009). Electoral rules, class coalitions and welfare state regimes, or how to explain Esping-Andersen with Stein Rokkan. *Socio-Economic Review*, 7(1):101–121.

Mitteregger, R. (2024). Socialized with "old cleavages" or "new dimensions": An Age-Period-Cohort analysis on electoral support in Western European multiparty systems (1949–2021). *Electoral Studies*, 87:102744.

Neundorf, A. and Adams, J. (2018). The micro-foundations of party competition and issue ownership: The reciprocal effects of citizens' issue salience and party attachments. *British Journal of Political Science*, 48(2):385–406.

Noël, A. and Thérien, J.-P. (2008). *Left and right in global politics*. Cambridge University Press.

Norris, P. and Inglehart, R. (2019). *Cultural backlash: Trump, Brexit, and authoritarian populism*. Cambridge University Press.

Oesch, D. and Rennwald, L. (2018). Electoral competition in Europe's new tripolar political space: Class voting for the left, centre-right and radical right. *European Journal of Political Research*, 57(4):783–807.

O'Grady, T. (2023). Is ideological polarisation by age group growing in Europe? *European Journal of Political Research*, 62(4): 1389–1402.

Oser, J., Hooghe, M., and Marien, S. (2013). Is online participation distinct from offline participation? A latent class analysis of participation types and their stratification. *Political Research Quarterly*, 66(1):91–101.

Rennwald, L. and Evans, G. (2014). When supply creates demand: Social democratic party strategies and the evolution of class voting. *West European Politics*, 37(5):1108–1135.

Rhodes-Purdy, M., Navarre, R., and Utych, S. (2023). *The age of discontent*. Cambridge University Press.

Roberts, M. E., Stewart, B. M., Tingley, D., et al. (2014). Structural topic models for open-ended survey responses. *American Journal of Political Science*, 58(4):1064–1082.

Rodden, J. A. (2019). *Why cities lose: The deep roots of the urban-rural political divide*. Basic Books.

Rodrik, D. and Stantcheva, S. (2021). A policy matrix for inclusive prosperity. *National Bureau of Economic Research*, w28736.

Rothschild, J. E., Howat, A. J., Shafranek, R. M., and Busby, E. C. (2019). Pigeonholing partisans: Stereotypes of party supporters and partisan polarization. *Political Behavior*, 41(2):423–443.

Schatz, E. (2009). Ethnographic immersion and the study of politics. In Schatz, E., editor, *Political ethnography: What immersion contributes to the study of politics*, pages 1–22. University of Chicago Press.

Seeberg, H. B. and Adams, J. (2024). Citizens' issue priorities respond to national conditions, less so to parties' issue emphases. *Working Paper*.

Sides, J., Tausanovitch, C., and Vavreck, L. (2022). *The bitter end: The 2020 presidential campaign and the challenge to American democracy*. Princeton University Press.

Sides, J., Tesler, M., and Vavreck, L. (2019). *Identity crisis: The 2016 presidential campaign and the battle for the meaning of America*. Princeton University Press.

Spies, D. and Franzmann, S. T. (2011). A two-dimensional approach to the political opportunity structure of extreme right parties in Western Europe. *West European Politics*, 34(5):1044–1069.

Spoon, J.-J. and Williams, C. J. (2021). "It's the economy, stupid": When new politics parties take on old politics issues. *West European Politics*, 44(4):802–824.

Stantcheva, S. (2022). Understanding of trade. *National Bureau of Economic Research*, w30040.

Stantcheva, S. (2024). Why do we dislike inflation? *National Bureau of Economic Research*, w32300.

Stenner, K. (2005). *The authoritarian dynamic*. Cambridge University Press.

Tichelbaecker, T., Gidron, N., Horne, W., and Adams, J. (2023). What do we measure when we measure affective polarization across countries? *Public Opinion Quarterly*, 87(3):803–815.

Van der Brug, W. and Van Spanje, J. (2009). Immigration, Europe and the "new" cultural dimension. *European Journal of Political Research*, 48(3):309–334.

Vicinanza, P., Goldberg, A., and Srivastava, S. B. (2023). A deep-learning model of prescient ideas demonstrates that they emerge from the periphery. *PNAS Nexus*, 2(1): pgac275.

Volkens, A., Krause, W., Lehmann, P., et al. (2017). The manifesto data collection: Manifesto project (mrg/cmp/marpor). Version 2017b. Berlin: Wissenschaftszentrum Berlin für sozialforschung (wzb). *Bron*, 1(1990):15.

Weyland, K. (2020). Populism's threat to democracy: Comparative lessons for the United States. *Perspectives on Politics*, 18(2):389–406.

Weyland, K. and Madrid, R. L. (2019). *When democracy trumps populism: European and Latin American lessons for the United States*. Cambridge University Press.

Zollinger, D. (2024). Cleavage identities in voters' own words: Harnessing open-ended survey responses. *American Journal of Political Science*, 68(1):139–59.

# Cambridge Elements ☰

# European Politics

## Catherine De Vries

*Bocconi University*

Catherine De Vries is a Dean of International Affairs and Professor of Political Science at Bocconi University. Her research revolves around some of the key challenges facing the European continent today, such as Euroscepticism, political fragmentation, migration and corruption. She has published widely in leading political science journals, including the American Political Science Review and the Annual Review of Political Science. She has published several books, including Euroscepticism and the Future of European integration (Oxford University Press), received the European Union Studies Association Best Book in EU Studies Award, and was listed in the Financial Times top-5 books to read about Europe's future.

## Gary Marks

*University of North Carolina at Chapel Hill and European University Institute*

Gary Marks is Burton Craige Professor at the University of North Carolina Chapel Hill, and Professor at the European University Institute, Florence. He has received the Humboldt Forschungspreis and the Daniel Elazar Distinguished Federalism Scholar Award. Marks has been awarded an Advanced European Research Council grant (2010–2015) and is currently senior researcher on a second Advanced European Research Council grant. He has published widely in leading political science journals, including the American Political Science Review and the American Journal of Political Science. Marks has published a dozen books, including A Theory of International Organization and Community, Scale and Regional Governance.

## About the Series

The Cambridge Elements Series in European Politics will provide a platform for cutting-edge comparative research on Europe at a time of rapid change for the disciplines of political science and international relations. The series is broadly defined, both in terms of subject and academic discipline. The thrust of the series will be thematic rather than ideographic. It will focus on studies that engage key elements of politics — e.g. how institutions work, how parties compete, how citizens participate in politics, how laws get made.

Printed in the United States
by Baker & Taylor Publisher Services